gettyimages
1950s

Decades of the 20th Century
Dekaden des 20. Jahrhunderts
Décennies du XXᵉ siècle

Nick Yapp

KÖNEMANN

This edition ©Tandem Verlag GmbH
KÖNEMANN is a trademark and an imprint of Tandem Verlag GmbH
Photographs ©1998 Getty Images

This book was produced by Getty Images
Unique House, 21–31 Woodfield Road, London W9 2BA

For KÖNEMANN: For Getty Images:
Managing editor: Sally Bald   Art director: Michael Rand
Project editor: Susanne Hergarden   Design: Ian Denning
German translation: Angela Ritter   Managing editor: Annabel Else
Contributing editor: Daniela Kumor   Picture editor: Ali Khoja
French translation: Francine Rey   Picture research: Alex Linghorn
Contributing editor: Stéphanie Aurin   Editor: James Hughes
                                          Proof reader: Elisabeth Ihre
                                          Scanning: Andy Cockayne
                                          Production: Robert Gray
                                          Special thanks: Leon Meyer,
                                          Téa Aganovic and Antonia Hille

Printed in China

ISBN 3-8331-1081-3

10 9 8 7 6 5 4 3
X IX VIII VII VI V IV III II I

Frontispiece: The 'American Dream' come true. In their uniform of
skirts, sweaters and sandals, crowned by little feathered hats, the
cream of wholesome American youth sip milkshakes in a drugstore in
the spring of 1950.

Frontispiz: Der „Amerikanische Traum" wird wahr. In Rock, Pulli,
Sandalen und federgeschmücktem Hütchen, der Einheitskleidung der
Creme der amerikanischen Jugend, genießen diese jungen Mädchen
ihre Milchshakes in einem Drugstore, Frühling 1950.

Frontispice: Le « rêve américain » se réalise. En jupe, tricot, sandales
et petits chapeaux à plumes, l'uniforme de la crème de la jeunesse
américaine saine, ces jeunes filles sirotent des milkshakes dans un
drugstore, printemps 1950.

Contents / Inhalt / Sommaire

Introduction

We'd 'never had it so good', in British prime minister Macmillan's election-winning phrase. In the West there were more houses, more cars, more fridges, vacuum cleaners, toasters, toys and trinkets than ever before. There was Rock 'n' Roll to blast our ears and the 3D film to hurt our eyes. In the lands of plenty all seemed set fair for boom time; the new supermarkets were stuffed with more wonders than Ali Baba's cave.

Elsewhere matters were neither set nor fair. A cold wind blew over Africa, Malaya, Cuba, Korea, Indochina. President Nasser of Egypt nationalized the Suez Canal, and he and Anthony Eden dealt a death blow to the old British Empire. Charles de Gaulle returned to power in France – some said to rescue her, some said to destroy her. Apartheid raised its hideously ugly head in South Africa. Stalin died, lamented by few of the millions who had been in his stern care.

There were changes almost everywhere. Abdullah of Jordan was assassinated, George VI and Eva Perón died, Leopold of the Belgians abdicated, the US Democrats were slaughtered at the polls. Most of the new rulers were greeted warmly. Elizabeth II was crowned with pomp and ceremony in a welter of admiration. Millions of Americans wore badges proclaiming 'I Like Ike'. Even Khrushchev was reckoned a vast improvement on his predecessor.

Nevertheless, there was a lot of anger about. The rebellious teenagers had their figurehead in the brief and brilliant career of James Dean. Righteous anger was mobilized by the American civil rights movement. White racists crawled out of the woodwork to engineer race riots in Britain and the United States – Little Rock and Notting Hill had their moments of ignominy. Mods clashed with rockers – usually on neutral territory. In the words of Jerry Lee Lewis, there was 'a whole lotta shakin' goin' on'.

There were wars in Korea and Tibet, risings in Hungary and East Berlin, civil wars in

Algeria and the Congo, and armed struggles for independence in Kenya and Cyprus. The patience of the old order was stretched almost to breaking point – it broke in the Sixties. The great powers succumbed to spy mania. In the United States the Rosenbergs were executed and Senator McCarthy began his villainous witch hunts. In Britain, among others, Burgess, MacLean and Philby vanished, to reappear after a disrespectful interval in Moscow.

Roger Bannister ran a mile in under four minutes. The sound barrier was broken. The first package holidays lured those born in a cold climate to have fun in the sun. The first generation of *kibbutzim* pioneered a new way of life in Israel. Disneyland opened. The 'teenager' arrived. The EEC was forged from the Iron and Steel Community of Europe.

The coffee bar and juke box were said to threaten the morals of the young and the wellbeing of society. The Hula Hoop strained the hips. Plastic replaced bakelite. Smokers enjoyed their last few puffs before rumours of a link with cancer spread like wildfire.

And God created Brigitte Bardot.

Einführung

„Noch nie ging es uns so gut", verkündete der britische Premierminister Macmillan nach seinem Wahlsieg. In Westeuropa gab es mehr Wohnungen, mehr Autos, mehr Kühlschränke, Staubsauger, Toaster, Spielzeug und Zierrat als je zuvor. Der Rock 'n' Roll strapazierte die Ohren und die 3-D-Filme die Augen. In den Ländern des Wohlstands schien nichts mehr dem Aufschwung im Wege zu stehen, die neuen Supermärkte bargen weit größere Schätze als Ali Babas Höhle.

Andernorts standen die Dinge nicht so gut. In Afrika, Malaya, Kuba, Korea und Indochina wehte ein weitaus eisigerer Wind. Der ägyptische Präsident Nasser verstaatlichte den Suezkanal und versetzte gemeinsam mit Anthony Eden dem alten Britischen Weltreich den Todesstoß. Charles de Gaulle kehrte an die Staatsspitze zurück, um – wie manche Stimmen meinten – Frankreich zu zerstören oder es zu retten. In Südafrika zeigte die Apartheid ihr schreckliches Gesicht. Stalin starb, kaum beweint von den Millionen von Menschen, die sein strenges Regime erlebt hatten.

Fast überall gab es Veränderungen. König Abdullah von Jordanien erlag einem Attentat, König Georg VI. und Eva Perón starben, der König von Belgien dankte ab, und die amerikanischen Demokraten erlitten eine schmähliche Wahlniederlage. Die meisten der neuen Herrscher wurden herzlich empfangen. Die Krönung Elisabeths II. wurde in Großbritannien prunkvoll begangen und begeistert gefeiert. Millionen von Amerikanern trugen Ansteckradeln mit dem Slogan „I Like Ike". Selbst Chruschtschow betrachtete man im Vergleich zu seinem Vorgänger als eine enorme Verbesserung.

Dennoch herrschte vielerorts Unmut und Zorn. Rebellierende Teenager fanden ihr Idol in James Dean und dessen kurzer wie brillanter Karriere. Die amerikanische Bürgerrechtsbewegung beschwor gerechten Zorn und Unterstützung für ihre Sache. Weiße Rassisten traten an die Öffentlichkeit und provozierten Rassenunruhen in Großbritannien und den

Vereinigten Staaten – Little Rock in Arkansas und der Londoner Stadtteil Notting Hill erlangten so bittere Berühmtheit. Mods und Rocker gerieten aneinander – meist auf neutralem Boden. „Alles wackelte ganz schön", wie Jerry Lee Lewis treffend formulierte.

Es gab Kriege in Korea und Tibet, Aufstände in Ungarn und Ost-Berlin, Bürgerkriege in Algerien und im Kongo sowie kriegerische Unabhängigkeitsbestrebungen in Kenia und auf Zypern. Die Geduld der alten Ordnung wurde einer harten Zerreißprobe unterworfen, der sie in den sechziger Jahren nachgeben mußte. Die Großmächte fahndeten nach Spionen: In den Vereinigten Staaten wurde das Ehepaar Rosenberg hingerichtet, und Senator McCarthy begann seine teuflischen Hexenjagden. Die britisch-russischen Doppelagenten Burgess, MacLean und Philby tauchten unter und setzten sich nach Moskau ab.

Roger Bannister lief eine Meile in weniger als vier Minuten. Die Schallmauer wurde durchbrochen. Die ersten Pauschalreiseangebote lockten die Menschen, die in einem weniger freundlichen Klima lebten, aus der Kälte in die Sonne. Die erste Generation von Kibbuzniks entwickelte einen neuen Lebensstil in Israel. Disneyland öffnete seine Pforten. Die „Teenager" kamen. Die Europäische Gemeinschaft für Kohle und Stahl gründete die EWG.

Cafés und Musikautomaten wurden als eine Gefahr für die Moral der Jugend und das Wohl der Gesellschaft angesehen. Der Hula-Hoop-Reifen beanspruchte die Hüften. Plastik ersetzte Bakelit. Raucher genossen ihre letzten Züge, bevor das Gerücht einer Verbindung zu Krebserkrankungen sich wie ein Lauffeuer verbreitete.

Und Gott schuf Brigitte Bardot.

Introduction

« Les temps n'ont jamais été aussi bons », telle fut la phrase prononcée par Macmillan, lors de son élection en tant que Premier ministre de Grande-Bretagne. Jamais auparavant, les pays occidentaux n'avaient connu une telle abondance de maisons, de voitures, de réfrigérateurs, d'aspirateurs, de grille-pains, de jouets et de gadgets. Le rock'n'roll abimait les oreilles et les films en trois dimensions les yeux. Dans les pays d'abondance, toutes les conditions semblaient réunies pour vivre une époque de grande prospérité. Les nouveaux supermarchés étaient remplis de plus de merveilles que la caverne d'Ali Baba.

Dans le reste du monde, les choses n'étaient ni réglées ni équitables. Un vent glacial soufflait sur l'Afrique, la Malaisie, Cuba, la Corée et l'Indochine. En Egypte, le président Nasser nationalisait le canal de Suez, l'intervention décidée par Anthony Eden porta un coup fatal au vieil Empire britannique. En France, Charles de Gaulle reprit le pouvoir – pour sauver le pays, selon certains, le faire courir à sa perte, selon d'autres. En Afrique du Sud, l'apartheid montrait son infâme visage. En URSS, parmi les millions de gens qui avaient vécu sous son sinistre régime, seule une petite minorité pleura la mort de Staline.

Un peu partout, une nouvelle époque se dessinait. Abdullah de Jordanie fut assassiné, Georges VI et Eva Perón moururent, Léopold de Belgique abdiqua et les démocrates américains subirent une défaite retentissante aux élections. Les nouveaux dirigeants étaient pour la plupart accueillis avec enthousiasme. Elisabeth II fut couronnée avec faste dans l'admiration générale. « I Like Ike », le badge de la campagne d'Eisenhower, fut porté par des millions d'Américains. Même Khrouchtchev, comparé à son prédécesseur, était synonyme de grands progrès.

Néanmoins, il y avait beaucoup de contestations dans l'air. Les « teen-agers » rebelles se reconnaissaient dans James Dean, dont la carrière fut aussi brève que brillante. Le mouvement des droits civiques américain engendra une vague d'indignation tandis que des racistes blancs provoquaient des émeutes raciales en Grande-Bretagne et aux Etats-Unis – Little Rock en Arkansas et le quartier londonien de Notting Hill devinrent ainsi tristement célèbres. Les Mods (garçons en scooter) et les Blousons noirs s'affrontaient, souvent en terrain neutre. Comme disait Jerry Lee Lewis, « ça secoue pas mal en ce moment ».

La guerre avait éclaté en Corée et au Tibet, ainsi que des soulèvements en Hongrie et à Berlin-Est, la guerre civile en Algérie et au Congo et des luttes armées pour l'indépendance au Kenya et à Chypre. La patience du pouvoir établi atteignait ses limites, pour succomber dans les années soixante. Les grandes puissances étaient en proie à l'espionnite. Aux Etats-Unis, les Rosenberg furent exécutés et le sénateur McCarthy entama son ignoble chasse aux sorcières. En Grande-Bretagne, les espions Burgess, MacLean et Philby, entre autres, disparurent avant de réapparaître, quelque temps plus tard, à Moscou.

Roger Bannister réussit à courir le mile en moins de quatre minutes. Le mur du son fut franchi. Les habitants des pays froids se laissaient séduire par les premières vacances organisées au soleil. En Israël, une nouvelle génération de kibboutz instaurait un nouveau style de vie. Disneyland ouvrit ses portes. L'ère des adolescents s'amorçait. La Communauté sidérurgique européenne fondait la CEE.

Les cafés et les juke-box étaient considérés comme une atteinte aux bonnes mœurs des jeunes et au bien-être de la société. Le hula hoop affinait les hanches. Le plastique remplaça la bakélite. Les fumeurs fumaient encore gaiement. La rumeur selon laquelle cigarette et cancer auraient un lien ne s'était pas encore répandue comme une traînée de poudre.

Et Dieu créa Brigitte Bardot.

1. Movers and shakers
Spieler und Gegenspieler
Progressistes et agitateurs

An unlikely entente. Fidel Castro and Richard Nixon shake
hands on 21 April 1959. Two months earlier, Castro had
become President of Cuba and proclaimed the Marxist-
Leninist revolution. Nixon was Eisenhower's vice-president
and a rabid anti-Communist.

Trügerische Eintracht. Händedruck zwischen Fidel Castro und
Richard Nixon am 21. April 1959. Zwei Monate zuvor hatte
Castro auf Kuba die marxistisch-leninistische Revolution
ausgerufen und die Regierungsgewalt übernommen. Nixon,
Vizepräsident der Vereinigten Staaten unter Eisenhower, war
ein erbitterter Gegner des Kommunismus.

Entente improbable. Poignée de mains entre Fidel Castro et
Richard Nixon, le 21 avril 1959. Deux mois plus tôt, Castro,
élu président du Conseil, avait proclamé la révolution
marxiste-léniniste à Cuba. Nixon, vice-président des Etats-Unis
sous Eisenhower, était un anti-communiste farouche.

1. Movers and shakers
Spieler und Gegenspieler
Progressistes et agitateurs

After the destruction and reconstruction of the Fourties, the world began to settle down. It was a new world, with a new problem. Never before had the entire planet been divided into two diametrically opposing camps. To the West, there was Capitalism, straining at the leash to swamp the market with bigger, better, shinier goods and prepared to crush anything that stood in its way. To the East, there was Stalinism, a hard-line corruption of communism, immovable, unpardoning and ferociously defensive. The two snarled at each other for most of the decade. Both had the bomb, both claimed they were prepared to use it.

The old men who had led the way in the Forties stumbled on into the Fifties. Churchill briefly returned as Britain's prime minister, Truman and Eisenhower in turn occupied the White House, Uncle Joe remained master of the Soviet Union until he died in 1953. In France, de Gaulle waited in the wings – his time was to come.

But there were immense political changes. France and Germany brokered the European Economic Community, in the belief that it could put an end to war in one continent at least. The old British Empire sickened and then dealt its own death blow in the folly of Suez. China scrambled into the 20th century. And Khrushchev smiled.

Nach der Zerstörung und dem Wiederaufbau in den vierziger Jahren begann sich das Leben wieder zu stabilisieren. Es war eine neue Welt, mit einem neuen Problem. Nie zuvor war der Planet in zwei diametral entgegengesetzte Lager gespalten gewesen. Im Westen herrschte der Kapitalismus, der den Markt mit immer größeren, besseren und attraktiveren Waren zu überschwemmen drohte, bereit alles niederzureißen, was ihm den Weg versperrte. Im Osten herrschte der Stalinismus, eine korrumpierte Form des Kommunismus, unbeweglich, gnadenlos und grimmig auf Verteidigung bedacht. Den größten Teil des Jahrzehnts über hielten sich diese Gegner in Schach. Beide verfügten über die Atombombe, beide verkündeten ihre Bereitschaft, sie erneut einzusetzen.

Die Herren, die bereits in den vierziger Jahren richtungsweisend waren, bestimmten auch in der folgenden Dekade die Politik. Churchill kehrte in Großbritannien für kurze Zeit als Premierminister zurück, während Truman und Eisenhower sich im Weißen Haus abwechselten. In der Sowjetunion behielt Josef Stalin bis zu seinem Tod 1953 die Zügel in der Hand. In Frankreich wartete de Gaulle auf seine große Stunde – sie sollte kommen.

Es gab tiefgreifende politische Veränderungen. Frankreich und Deutschland forcierten die Europäische Wirtschaftsgemeinschaft und hofften, daß damit dem Kontinent kein Krieg mehr drohte. Das kränkelnde alte Britische Weltreich versetzte sich mit der Suez-Krise selbst den Todesstoß. China stolperte ins 20. Jahrhundert. Und Chruschtschow lächelte.

Après la destruction et la reconstruction des années quarante, le monde se stabilisa quelque peu. C'était un monde nouveau, face à un problème nouveau. Jamais auparavant, la planète n'avait été divisée en deux camps diamétralement opposés. A l'Ouest régnait un capitalisme en pleine expansion, qui inondait le marché de biens de consommation toujours plus grands, de meilleure qualité et plus clinquants, prêt à écraser tout ce qui se mettrait en travers de sa route. A l'Est sévissait le stalinisme, une version très éloignée du communisme, inflexible, impitoyable et férocement sur la défensive. Ces deux camps se défièrent tout au long de la décennie. Tous les deux détenaient la bombe atomique, tous les deux se déclaraient prêts à l'utiliser.

Les hommes qui avaient su montrer le chemin dans les années quarante entrèrent en trébuchant dans les années cinquante. Churchill fut de nouveau Premier ministre mais pour une courte durée, Truman et Eisenhower entrèrent l'un après l'autre à la Maison Blanche et Staline resta le maître de l'Union soviétique jusqu'à sa mort, en 1953. En France, de Gaulle attendait dans l'anti-chambre du pouvoir – son heure arrivait.

Il y eut d'énormes bouleversements politiques. La France et l'Allemagne furent les principaux acteurs de la Communauté économique européenne, dans l'espoir de mettre un terme définitif à la guerre, du moins sur le continent européen. Le vieil Empire britannique malade s'infligea lui-même un coup fatal en intervenant dans l'affaire du canal de Suez. La Chine bascula dans le XXe siècle. Et Khrouchtchev souriait.

Josef Stalin lies in state in the Hall of Columns, Trade Union House, Moscow, 12 March 1953. He had died one week earlier. The burial commission decreed: 'Comrade Stalin's body must be laid in the coffin in military uniform, with the medals of Hero of the Soviet Union and Hero of Socialist labour… in gold.'

Josef Stalin wird eine Woche nach seinem Tod in der Säulenhalle des Moskauer Gewerkschaftssitzes aufgebahrt, 12. März 1953. Die Beerdigungskommission verfügte zu den Trauerfeierlichkeiten: „Kamerad Stalins Leichnam soll in militärischer Uniform beigesetzt und mit den goldenen Orden Held der Sowjetunion und Held der sozialistischen Arbeit geschmückt werden."

Joseph Staline, encore exposé dans la salle des colonnes de la Maison des syndicats, une semaine après sa mort, Moscou, le 12 mars 1953. Selon le décret de la commission chargée des funérailles, « le corps du camarade Staline doit reposer dans son cercueil, vêtu de son uniforme militaire et décoré de ses médailles de héros de l'Union soviétique et de héros du travail socialiste… en or ».

Nikolai Bulganin (left) and Nikita Khrushchev at the Cenotaph, London, April 1956. They had just laid wreaths at the memorial to the dead of two world wars.

Nikolai Bulganin (links) und Nikita Chruschtschow vor dem Londoner Ehrenmal, April 1956. Sie hatten dort Kränze zum Gedenken an die Opfer der beiden Weltkriege niedergelegt.

Nikolaï Boulganine (à gauche) et Nikita Khrouchtchev au Cénotaphe de Londres, avril 1956, après avoir déposé une gerbe devant le monument aux morts des deux guerres mondiales.

Nikita Khrushchev waves to crowds in a Prague street during a public
relations visit to Czechoslovakia, July 1957. On Khrushchev's right is the
Czech President, Zápotocký. Waving in the car behind is Nikolai Bulganin.

Nikita Chruschtschow grüßt die Menschenmengen in Prag während eines
Staatsbesuchs in der Tschechoslowakei, Juli 1957. Zu seiner Rechten sitzt
der tschechische Präsident Zápotocký. Im nachfolgenden Wagen winkt
stehend Nikolai Bulganin.

Nikita Khrouchtchev salue la foule dans une rue de Prague lors d'une
visite officielle en Tchécoslovaquie, juillet 1957. Le président tchèque,
Zápotocký, est assis à la droite de Khrouchtchev. Dans la voiture qui suit,
se tient Nikolaï Boulganine saluant lui aussi la foule.

Josip Broz, better known as Tito, President of the Yugoslav Federal Republic, 1953. To many in the West, Tito was a non-aligned Communist hero.

Josip Broz, besser bekannt unter dem Namen Tito, Präsident der Föderativen Volksrepublik Jugoslawien, 1953. In westlichen Kreisen galt Tito als bündnisfreier kommunistischer Held.

Josip Broz, mieux connu sous le nom de Tito, président de la République fédérale de Yougoslavie, 1953. Nombreux étaient ceux qui, à l'Ouest, voyaient en Tito un héros communiste refusant de s'aligner.

The Argentinian-born revolutionary leader, Che Guevara, 1952. The picture was taken during the Cuban battle of Santa Clara, following Batista's coup.

Der aus Argentinien stammende Revolutionär Che Guevara, 1952. Diese Aufnahme entstand nach General Batistas Staatsstreich, während der Schlacht um Santa Clara auf Kuba.

Che Guevara, le révolutionnaire d'origine argentine, 1952. Ce cliché fut pris à Cuba durant la bataille de Santa Clara, après le putsch de Batista.

Fidel Castro, leader of the Communist revolution in Cuba during the late Fifties, relaxes on a sugar plantation near Havana. Castro's father was a sugar planter, his brother Raúl another ardent revolutionary.

Fidel Castro, der in den späten fünfziger Jahren die kommunistische Revolution auf Kuba anführte, entspannt sich auf einer Zuckerrohrplantage bei Havanna. Castros Vater baute Zuckerrohr an, sein Bruder Raúl war ein glühender Revolutionär.

Fidel Castro, leader de la révolution communiste à la fin des années cinquante, se détend dans une plantation de sucre près de La Havane, Cuba. Le père de Castro était planteur de sucre et son frère Raúl un ardent révolutionnaire.

Ho Chi Minh, November 1950. During the late Forties and
early Fifties, Ho was directing military operations against the
French in Vietnam.

Ho Chi Minh, November 1950. In den späten vierziger und
den frühen fünfziger Jahren leitete Ho militärische
Operationen gegen die Franzosen in Vietnam.

Hô Chi Minh, novembre 1950. De la fin des années quarante
au début des années cinquante, Hô dirigea les opérations
militaires menées contre les Français au Vietnam.

The first prime minister of India, Jawaharlal Nehru, is guest of honour
at an official dinner in Vietnam, 1954. It was the year French troops were reluctantly
evacuated from Vietnam after the victories of the Viet Minh.

Der erste indische Ministerpräsident, Jawaharlal Nehru, ist Ehrengast bei einem
Staatsempfang in Vietnam, 1954. In jenem Jahr hatten die siegreichen Vietminh-
Soldaten die französischen Truppen zum Abzug aus Vietnam gezwungen.

Le premier Premier ministre de l'Inde, Jawaharlal Nehru, invité d'honneur d'un dîner
officiel au Vietnam, 1954. Cette année-là, les troupes françaises durent se résigner à
évacuer le Vietnam après la victoire des Viêt-Minh.

Delegates at the NATO Conference in Paris, 19
December 1957. (From left) Van Acker (Belgium),
Dieffenbaker (Canada), Hansen (Denmark),
Gaillard (France), Adenauer (West Germany),
Karamanlis (Greece), Jonasson (Iceland), Zoli
(Italy), Spaak (NATO Secretary-General), Bech
(Chairman), Hommel (Luxembourg), Luns
(Netherlands), Gerhardsen (Norway), Cunha
(Portugal), Menderes (Turkey), Macmillan (Britain),
Eisenhower (USA).

Delegierte der Pariser NATO-Konferenz,
19. Dezember 1957. (Von links) Van Acker
(Belgien), Dieffenbaker (Kanada), Gaillard
(Frankreich), Adenauer (BRD), Hansen
(Dänemark), Karamanlis (Griechenland), Jonasson
(Island), Zoli (Italien), Spaak (Generalsekretär der
NATO), Bech (Vorsitzender), Hommel
(Luxemburg), Luns (Niederlande), Gerhardsen
(Norwegen), Cunha (Portugal), Menderes (Türkei),
Macmillan (Großbritannien), Eisenhower (USA).

Délégués à la conférence de l'Otan à Paris,
19 décembre 1957. (De gauche à droite) Van Acker
(Belgique), Dieffenbaker (Canada), Gaillard
(France), Adenauer (Allemagne de l'Ouest), Hansen
(Danemark), Karamanlis (Grèce), Jonasson
(Islande), Zoli (Italie), Spaak (secrétaire général de
l'Otan), Bech (président), Hommel (Luxembourg),
Luns (Pays-Bas), Gerhardsen (Norvège), Cunha
(Portugal), Menderes (Turquie), Macmillan
(Grande-Bretagne), Eisenhower (USA).

The Senator from Wisconsin, Joseph McCarthy, at the height of his power in 1953. McCarthy instigated witch-hunts of 'Reds' and accused Truman's administration of 'crawling with Communists'. The following year he was condemned by the US Senate for conduct unbecoming to a Senator. He died in May 1957.

Der Senator aus Wisconsin, Joseph McCarthy, auf dem Höhepunkt seiner Macht, 1953. McCarthy initiierte eine Hexenjagd auf „die Roten" und beschuldigte Präsident Trumans Regierung, „von Kommunisten durchsetzt zu sein". Ein Jahr später wurde sein Verhalten vom amerikanischen Senat als eines Senatoren unwürdig verurteilt. Er starb im Mai 1957.

Le sénateur du Wisconsin, Joseph McCarthy, au sommet de sa gloire en 1953. Il avait lancé la chasse aux sorcières contre les « Rouges » et accusé l'administration Truman de « frayer avec les communistes ». Le Sénat le condamna en 1954 pour ses prises de position indignes d'un sénateur. Il mourut en mai 1957.

Crusader in a plastic mac. US evangelist Billy Graham proclaims his message of salvation at the White City in London, 1954.

Ein Kreuzritter im Regenmantel. Der amerikanische Prediger Billy Graham verkündet im Londoner Stadion White City seine Botschaft der Erlösung, 1954.

Croisade en imperméable. L'évangéliste américain Billy Graham délivre son message de salut au stade White City de Londres, 1954.

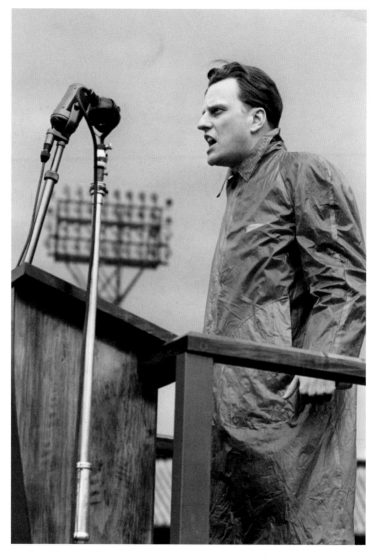

Man with a mission, One: John Edgar Hoover sits at his desk in 1950. He remained in charge of the Federal Bureau of Investigation from 1924 until his death in 1972. During that time, his targets ranged from mobsters and racketeers to gays and liberal activists.

Ein Mann mit einem Auftrag, Szene 1: John Edgar Hoover 1950 an seinem Schreibtisch. Von 1924 bis zu seinem Tod 1972 unterstand ihm das FBI. Während dieser Zeit setzte er seine Männer nicht nur auf Gauner und Gangster, sondern auch auf Homosexuelle und liberale Aktivisten an.

Un homme et sa mission (1): John Edgar Hoover à son bureau en 1950. Il dirigea le FBI de 1924 à 1972, année de sa mort. Pendant toute cette période, il s'en prit essentiellement aux truands et aux racketteurs, aux homosexuels et aux militants de gauche.

Man with a mission, Two: Malcolm X at a Black Muslim rally in Newark, New Jersey in 1955. Behind him is the 'Messenger of Allah' (Elijah Mohammed), the man who converted the former Malcolm Little to the Muslim faith.

Ein Mann mit einem Auftrag, Szene 2: Malcolm X auf einer Versammlung schwarzer Muslime in Newark, New Jersey, 1955. Unmittelbar hinter ihm sitzt der „Botschafter Allahs" (Elijah Mohammed), der den früheren Malcolm Little zum mohammedanischen Glauben bekehrt hatte.

Un homme et sa mission (2) : Malcolm X à un rassemblement des Black Muslim à Newark, New Jersey, 1955. Derrière lui est assis le « messager d'Allah» (Elijah Mohammed), l'homme qui convertit l'ex-Malcolm Little à l'islam.

'There is something in the soul that cries out for freedom…' Martin Luther King Jr. addresses the masses gathered on the Mall in Washington DC during the Prayer Pilgrimage, 17 May 1957.

„Etwas in der Seele schreit nach Unabhängigkeit …" Martin Luther King Jr. spricht während einer Wallfahrt zu den Massen in Washington D.C., 17. Mai 1957.

« Il y a quelque chose dans l'âme qui crie pour la Liberté… ». Martin Luther King Jr. s'adresse à la foule rassemblée sur la promenade à Washington D.C. lors du Pélerinage de la prière, le 17 mai 1957.

Republican presidential candidate Dwight D Eisenhower (right) with his running-mate Richard Nixon (centre) leaving their campaign headquarters, November 1952. With them is Arthur Summerfield, Chairman of the Republican National Committee.

Dwight D. Eisenhower (rechts), Präsidentschaftskandidat der Republikanischen Partei, und Richard Nixon (Mitte), Kandidat für die Vizepräsidentschaft, verlassen in Begleitung des Vorsitzenden des Nationalkomitees der Republikaner, Arthur Summerfield, die Wahlkampfzentrale, November 1952.

Dwight D. Eisenhower (à droite), le candidat républicain à la présidence, et son colistier Richard Nixon (au centre) quittent le quartier général de la campagne, accompagnés d'Arthur Summerfield, président du Comité national des républicains, novembre 1952.

'We Like Ike.' Supporters of Eisenhower at his re-election rally in Madison Square Garden, November 1956. Four days later Eisenhower returned to the White House after a landslide victory, again over Adlai Stevenson.

„We Like Ike." Eisenhower-Anhänger bei einer Wahlversammlung im Madison Square Garden, November 1956. Vier Tage später kehrte Eisenhower nach einem erneuten überwältigenden Wahlsieg über Adlai Stevenson ins Weiße Haus zurück.

« We Like Ike. » Supporteurs d'Eisenhower participant au meeting électoral de Madison Square Garden, novembre 1956. Quatre jours plus tard, Eisenhower retournait à la Maison Blanche après avoir remporté une nouvelle victoire écrasante sur Adlai Stevenson.

Secretary of State John Foster Dulles (right, in wheelchair) with Winston Churchill and President Eisenhower, May 1959. Four days later, Dulles died of cancer. He was renowned for his brinkmanship, the fine art of almost going to war.

Außenminister John Foster Dulles (rechts, im Rollstuhl) mit Winston Churchill und Präsident Eisenhower, Mai 1959. Vier Tage später erlag Dulles einem Krebsleiden. Er war berühmt gewesen für sein Spiel mit dem Feuer, nämlich die Kunst, beinahe den Krieg zu erklären.

Le secrétaire d'Etat John Foster Dulles (à droite, en chaise roulante) avec Winston Churchill et le président Eisenhower, mai 1959. Quatre jours plus tard, Dulles mourait d'un cancer. C'était un stratège réputé de la corde raide, sachant user de la menace de guerre quand il le fallait.

Young members of the Kennedy Clan in 1955. (From left to right) Robert Francis Kennedy, Edward Moore Kennedy and John Fitzgerald Kennedy. JFK was already the Democrat Senator for Massachusetts, but fate had much in store for all three.

Die jungen Mitglieder des Kennedy-Clans, 1955. (Von links nach rechts) Robert Francis Kennedy, Edward Moore Kennedy und John Fitzgerald Kennedy. JFK war bereits demokratischer Senator von Massachusetts. Aber das Rad des Schicksals sollte sich für jeden von ihnen noch weiter drehen.

Les jeunes membres du clan Kennedy, 1955. (De gauche à droite) Robert Francis Kennedy, Edward Moore Kennedy et John Fitzgerald Kennedy. J. F. K. était déjà le sénateur démocrate du Massachusetts. Le destin des trois hommes était encore loin d'être joué.

Winston Churchill, with his wife, gives the Victory 'V' sign from Conservative Party headquarters, South Woodford, October 1951. Three weeks later, he was prime minister.

Winston Churchill mit seiner Ehefrau, Oktober 1951. Er zeigt sich in der Wahlzentrale der Konservativen Partei in South Woodford siegessicher. Drei Wochen später wurde er Premier-minister.

Winston Churchill accompagné de sa femme fait le « V » de la victoire au siège du parti conservateur, South Woodford, octobre 1951. Trois semaines plus tard, il était élu Premier ministre.

Margaret Roberts
(later Mrs Thatcher)
canvasses during her
general election
campaign in
Dartford, England,
1951. She lost.

Margaret Roberts
(die spätere Mrs.
Thatcher) auf
Stimmenfang wäh-
rend der Parlaments-
wahlen, Dartford,
England, 1951. Sie
verlor.

Margaret Roberts
(future madame
Thatcher) en cam-
pagne pendant les
élections législatives
à Dartford, Angle-
terre, 1951. Elle
les perdit.

The actor in the wings. Ronald and Nancy Reagan at a dinner in 1952. It was the year of their marriage. Reagan was already president of the Screen Actors' Guild.

Der Schauspieler, der auf seinen großen Auftritt wartet. Ronald und Nancy Reagan im Jahr ihrer Hochzeit, 1952. Reagan war zu jener Zeit bereits Präsident der Vereinigung der Filmschauspieler.

L'acteur en coulisses. Ronald et Nancy Reagan à un dîner en 1952, année de leur mariage. Reagan était déjà le président de la société des acteurs de cinéma.

Dr Zeki Djabi of Syria presents an award to Eva Perón, wife of the Argentinian President, at a ceremony in the Casa de Gobiemo, Buenos Aires, April 1952.

Dr. Zeki Dschabi aus Syrien überreicht Eva Perón, der Gattin des argentinischen Präsidenten, eine Auszeichnung während einer Zeremonie in der Casa de Gobiemo, Buenos Aires, April 1952.

Le Dr. Zeki Djabi de Syrie remet une récompense à Eva Perón, épouse du président argentin, lors d'une cérémonie tenue à la Casa de Gobiemo, Buenos Aires, avril 1952.

Princess Elizabeth and the Duke of Edinburgh leave Montreal on the Royal Train bound for Quebec, during their tour of Canada, October 1951. Later they crossed the border and appeared on US television, billed as 'the heiress presumptive to the throne and her sailor husband'.

Prinzessin Elisabeth und der Herzog von Edinburgh verlassen mit der Königlichen Eisenbahn Montreal, um nach Quebec zu gelangen, Oktober 1951. Während ihrer Kanadareise überquerten sie auch die Grenze der Vereinigten Staaten. Im amerikanischen Fernsehen nannte man sie „die designierte Thronfolgerin und ihr Ehemann, der Matrose".

La princesse Elisabeth et le duc d'Edimbourg, en visite au Canada, quittent Montréal pour Québec à bord du train royal, octobre 1951. Ils se rendirent ensuite aux Etats-Unis où la télévision américaine les présenta comme « l'héritière présomptive du trône et son mari, le marin ».

Edward, Duke of
Windsor, chats to
Baroness de Cabrol,
Paris, December
1954. The theme,
pre-revolutionary
Russia, must have
brought a tear to
many an eye.

Eduard, Herzog von
Windsor, im Ge-
spräch mit Baronin
von Cabrol, Paris,
Dezember 1954.
Das Thema jenes
Abends, das vor-
revolutionäre Ruß-
land, hat sicherlich
einige Gemüter
bewegt.

Edouard, duc de
Windsor, échange
quelques mots avec
la baronne de
Cabrol, Paris,
décembre 1954. Le
thème de la soirée,
la Russie pré-
révolutionnaire, dut
mettre la larme à
l'œil à plus
d'un convive.

2. Conflict
Konflikte
Conflits

In late October 1956 Hungarian police fired at a crowd
demonstrating outside a radio station. Here Soviet tanks
rumble into Budapest on 27 October as the struggle for
Hungary begins. It lasted barely a month.

Ende Oktober 1956 schoß die ungarische Polizei auf eine
Menschenmenge, die vor einem Radiosender demonstrierte.
Diese Aufnahme vom 27. Oktober zeigt sowjetische Panzer in
den Straßen von Budapest. Der Kampf um Ungarn sollte
kaum einen Monat dauern.

A la fin octobre 1956, la police hongroise tira sur une foule
de manifestants réunie devant les locaux d'une station de
radio. Le 27 octobre des chars soviétiques entrèrent dans
Budapest alors que le mouvement insurrectionnel commençait. Il dura un mois à peine.

2. Conflict
   Konflikte
   Conflits

It was one of the most violent decades of all time, lacking only the homogeneity of world war to be perhaps the worst. There was bloodshed and fighting in Asia, Africa, Europe, Central America and the Middle East. Almost all the struggles were fuelled by the desire of native peoples to be free of colonial rule, the one exception being the Korean War. However much the West insisted that the initiative to invade Korea had come from the United Nations, this was a war between Capitalism and Communism.

The Soviet Union clung more successfully to their European empire, though it cost them dear in friends and members of the communist parties internationally.

The British found themselves fighting imperial rearguard actions in Kenya, Malaya, Cyprus and points east. As if this wasn't enough, the Conservative government launched one of the most inept and inexcusable invasions of all time when they precipitated the Suez Crisis.

In Indochina the French held a full scale rehearsal for the Vietnam war 20 years later. They were defeated by the same people under the same leader in the same way as the Americans were to be. There are few tragedies greater than the inability of politicians to learn the lessons of history.

Die fünfziger Jahre standen im Zeichen der Gewalt wie kaum eine andere Dekade – es fehlte ihnen lediglich ein Weltkrieg. Kämpfe und Blutvergießen dominierten das Leben in Asien, Afrika, Europa, Mittelamerika und dem Nahen Osten. Beinahe alle Auseinandersetzungen entstanden aus dem Wunsch der Kolonialvölker, sich endlich der Fremdherrschaft zu entledigen. Die einzige Ausnahme bildete der Krieg in Korea. So sehr der Westen auch darauf beharrte, daß die Vereinten Nationen die Invasion Koreas initiiert hätten, war dies doch ganz unverkennbar ein Krieg zwischen Kapitalismus und Kommunismus.

Die Sowjetunion behielt ihr europäisches Reich mit Erfolg in der Hand, obwohl sie dies mit einem Verlust an Freunden und Mitgliedern der kommunistischen Parteien auf internationaler Ebene teuer bezahlen mußte.

Das britische Empire sah sich unvermittelt mit Nachhutgefechten in Kenia, Malaya, Zypern und östlichen Gebieten konfrontiert. Doch als wäre dies nicht genug, leitete die konservative Regierung eine der ungeschicktesten und unverzeihlichsten Invasionen in die Wege, die es je gab, und beschwor damit die Suez-Krise herauf.

In Indochina erlebten die Franzosen eine Art Generalprobe für den 20 Jahre später folgenden Vietnamkrieg. Sie wurden von denselben Männern, denselben Kommandanten und auf dieselbe Weise wie später die Amerikaner besiegt. Es gibt wohl kaum etwas Tragischeres als die Unfähigkeit von Politikern, aus der Geschichte zu lernen.

Cette décennie fut l'une des plus violentes de l'histoire, exception faite des deux guerres mondiales dont l'horreur fut concentrée dans le temps. Le sang coulait lors de combats incessants en Asie, en Afrique, en Europe, en Amérique centrale et au Moyen-Orient. Ces luttes étaient pour la plupart nourries du désir des peuples de se libérer du joug colonial, la seule exception étant la guerre de Corée. Pourtant, de l'avis de nombreux dirigeants occidentaux, l'invasion de la Corée avait été décidée par les Nations unies, motivée par la guerre idéologique que se livraient capitalistes et communistes.

L'Union soviétique dominait avec succès son Empire européen, au risque de perdre de nombreux alliés et adhérents communistes sur le plan international.

Les Britanniques se trouvèrent impliqués, au nom de l'Empire, dans des actions de combats d'arrière-garde au Kenya, en Malaisie, à Chypre et dans plusieurs régions de l'Est. Comme si cela ne suffisait pas, le gouvernement conservateur lança l'une des invasions les plus inefficaces et les plus inexcusables de tous les temps en intervenant dans la crise du canal de Suez.

En Indochine, les Français étaient engagés dans une guerre qui se répéterait moins de vingt ans plus tard avec la guerre du Vietnam. Ils furent vaincus par les mêmes hommes, le même dirigeant et les mêmes tactiques qui viendraient à bout des Américains. Il n'y a guère plus tragique que l'incapacité des politiciens à tirer des leçons de l'histoire.

Bert Hardy's photograph of US Marines making their assault on the Korean port of Inchon, 1 October 1950. They suffered no casualties that day, but conditions were appalling.

Diese Aufnahme von Bert Hardy zeigt amerikanische Marinesoldaten beim Angriff auf den koreanischen Hafen Inchon, 1. Oktober 1950. An jenem Tag erlitt die Truppe zwar keine Verluste, doch die ungünstigen Umstände erschwerten die Aktion.

Cliché de Bert Hardy pris lors de l'assaut du port coréen d'Inchon par les Marines américains, 1er octobre 1950. Il n'y eut aucune victime ce jour-là mais, les combats furent terribles.

Refugees fleeing
from a war zone in
Korea, 16 September
1950. The war
began in June, and
the North Koreans
swept southwards
unhindered.

Flüchtlinge in einem
Kriegsgebiet in
Korea, 16. Septem-
ber 1950. Der Krieg
hatte im Juni be-
gonnen, und die
Nordkoreaner
drangen ungehindert
in den Süden vor.

Réfugiés fuyant une
zone de combats,
Corée, 16 septembre
1950. La guerre
débuta en juin et des
vagues de Nord-
Coréens affluèrent
vers la frontière Sud
qu'ils purent fran-
chir librement.

A member of the
US 1st Marine
division flushes out
sniper positions
with a flame
thrower, 1952.
By then, North
Korean troops had
been pushed back to
the 38th Parallel.

Ein Soldat der 1. US-
Marinedivision treibt
Heckenschützen mit
einem Flammen-
werfer aus ihrem
Versteck, 1952. Zu
jener Zeit waren die
nordkoreanischen
Truppen bereits bis
zum 38. Breitengrad
zurückgedrängt
worden.

Un Marine améri-
cain du 1er corps
tire au lance-
flammes sur les
positions de tireurs
isolés, 1952. Les
troupes nord-
coréennes avaient
été repoussées en
retrait du 38^{e}
parallèle.

A civilian casualty reaches the beach during the Inchon landings and invasion, 1950. Thousands of civilians were made homeless by the war, innocent victims of a conflict that few understood. The assault craft used by the Americans can be seen in the background.

Kriegsopfer am Strand von Inchon, 1950. Tausende von Zivilisten verloren durch den Krieg ihr Heim und wurden unschuldige Opfer eines Konflikts, dessen Ursachen kaum jemand verstand. Das amerikanische Kriegsschiff für die Invasion ist im Hintergrund zu erkennen.

Cette femme, blessée lors du débarquement dans le port d'Inchon, est évacuée vers la plage, 1950. Cette guerre fit des milliers de sans-abris, victimes innocentes d'un conflit dont le sens échappait à la plupart. A l'arrière-plan, les navires utilisés par les Américains pendant l'assaut.

A group of North Korean prisoners of war, 7 October 1950. The US landings at Inchon, some 200 miles behind the front line, had taken the North Koreans by surprise. Prisoners from both sides were harshly treated, and many photographs were suppressed.

Nordkoreanische Kriegsgefangene, 7. Oktober 1950. Die Landung der Amerikaner in Inchon, das etwa 320 km hinter der Front lag, hatte die Nordkoreaner überrascht. Mit Gefangenen wurde auf beiden Seiten hart umgegangen, und viele Fotoreportagen wurden zensiert.

Prisonniers de guerre nord-coréens, 7 octobre 1950. Le débarquement des Américains à Inchon, à quelque 320 km de la ligne de front, prit les Nord-Coréens par surprise. Les prisonniers furent maltraités dans les deux camps et de nombreux clichés censurés.

After the landings. An American soldier patrols one of the streets of Inchon, October 1950. The invasion had been preceded by two days of air strikes and bombardment by US cruisers and destroyers, which had destroyed most of the city.

Nach der Landung. Ein amerikanischer Soldat patrouilliert durch eine Straße in Inchon, Oktober 1950. Der Invasion waren zweitägige Luftangriffe und Bombardierungen durch die Kreuzer und Zerstörer der US-Marine vorausgegangen, die den größten Teil der Stadt in Schutt und Asche legten.

Après le débarquement. Un soldat américain patrouille dans une rue d'Inchon, octobre 1950. L'invasion fut précédée, deux jours durant, de raids aériens et de bombardements par la flotte américaine, qui détruisirent presque entièrement la ville.

Members of the French infantry fight to hold on to their colonial presence in South-East Asia during the Indochina War of 1946 to 1954. The original caption for this picture suggested that the Viet Minh 'rebels' were being destroyed – it wasn't so.

Soldaten der französischen Infanterie versuchten ihre koloniale Präsenz in Südostasien während des Krieges in Indochina von 1946 bis 1954 zu wahren. Die ursprüngliche Bildunterschrift zu dieser Aufnahme legte nahe, daß der Aufstand der Vietminh-„Rebellen" niedergeschlagen wurde – dem war nicht so.

Des soldats de l'infanterie française au combat pour défendre leur présence coloniale dans le Sud-Est asiatique pendant la guerre d'Indochine, de 1946 à 1954. La légende originale de ce cliché laissait croire que les « rebelles » Viêt-Minh avaient été vaincus – c'était faux.

Local civilians flee in panic along the streets of Saigon during fighting in Vietnam's civil war, May 1956. Not until 1973 did their suffering end.

Während des Vietnamkrieges, Mai 1956 laufen Zivilisten in Panik durch die Straßen Saigons. Ihre Leiden sollten erst 1973 enden.

Des civils paniqués fuient dans les rues de Saïgon durant une attaque, en pleine guerre du Viêt Nam, mai 1956. Il faudra attendre 1973 pour qu'un terme soit mis à leurs souffrances.

Demonstrators mass together outside Government House, Algiers, 23 May 1958. According to General Jacques Massu only one man was capable of ensuring 'the everlastingness of French Algeria' – Charles de Gaulle. Four years later, de Gaulle granted Algerian independence.

Demonstranten versammeln sich vor dem Regierungsgebäude in Algier, 23. Mai 1958. Laut General Jacques Massu war es nur einem Mann möglich, die „Unvergänglichkeit eines französischen Algeriens" sicherzustellen – Charles de Gaulle. Vier Jahre später jedoch gewährte de Gaulle Algerien die Unabhängigkeit.

Manifestants réunis devant la Maison du gouverneur, Alger, le 23 mai 1958. Pour le général Jacques Massu, un seul homme pouvait garantir la « pérennité de l'Algérie française » – Charles de Gaulle. Quatre ans plus tard, de Gaulle accordait l'indépendance à l'Algérie.

Generals Raoul
Salan (left, in kepi)
and Jacques Massu
(in beret) at the
monument to the
Unknown Warrior,
Algiers, 1958.
They were later
imprisoned for their
work in the OAS
(organisation armée
secrète).

Die Generäle Raoul
Salan (links, mit
Käppi) und Jacques
Massu (mit Basken-
mütze) am Ehrenmal
des Unbekannten
Soldaten in Algier,
1958. Später
mußten sie für ihre
Arbeit in der OAS
(organisation armée
secrète).

Les généraux Raoul
Salan (à gauche,
avec le képi) et
Jacques Massu (en
béret) devant le
monument du soldat
inconnu, Alger,
1958. Ils furent par
la suite emprisonnés
pour leurs
agissements au sein
de l'OAS
(organisation armée
secrète).

Twilight of the Empire, 1953. A wounded member of the Special Air Service is evacuated by helicopter during the Malayan Emergency. For 12 years, from 1948 to 1960, the old British order was maintained by young British blood in faraway jungles.

Abenddämmerung des Britischen Weltreiches, 1953. Ein verletzter Soldat der britischen Luftwaffe wird während des Malaiischen Aufstands auf den Inseln mit einem Hubschrauber evakuiert. Von 1948 bis 1960 wurde die alte britische Weltordnung in abgelegenen Dschungel nur unter Einsatz junger Briten aufrechterhalten.

Le crépuscule de l'Empire, 1953. Un soldat des SAS, blessé, est évacué par hélicoptère durant le conflit malaisien. Pendant douze ans, de 1948 à 1960, l'Empire britannique survécut grâce au sang versé par toute une jeune génération de Britanniques qui dut combattre dans de lointaines jungles.

A British soldier uses his cigarette to burn leeches off the back of a comrade, somewhere in Malaya, 20 June 1953.

Ein britischer Soldat entfernt mit einer Zigarette Blutegel vom Rücken eines Kameraden, irgendwo in Malaya, 20. Juni 1953.

Un soldat britannique se sert de sa cigarette pour brûler les sangsues, collées sur le dos d'un camarade, quelque part en Malaisie, 20 juin 1953.

Soldiers from the South Staffordshire Regiment close the Turkish quarter of Nicosia, Cyprus, September 1955. Trouble was expected during the trial of a local for killing a Turkish Cypriot policeman.

Soldaten des Regiments von South Staffordshire riegeln das türkische Viertel von Nikosia auf Zypern mit Stacheldraht ab, September 1955. Für die Zeit der Gerichtsverhandlung gegen einen griechischen Zyprioten, der einen türkisch-zypriotischen Polizisten ermordet hatte, wurde mit Unruhen gerechnet.

Des soldats du régiment de South Staffordshire bouclent le quartier turc de Nicosie pour parer à d'éventuelles émeutes pendant le procès d'un habitant de la ville, jugé pour avoir tué un policier chypriote turc, septembre 1955, Chypre.

A woman weeps in the village of Kontemenos during the Cypriot war of independence, 16 June 1958. The occasion was the funeral of five Greek Cypriots killed in nationalist unrest.

Eine weinende Frau bei einer Beerdigung in dem zyprischen Dorf Kontemenos, 16. Juni 1958. Hier wurden fünf griechische Zyprioten beigesetzt, die im Unabhängigkeitskrieg ums Leben gekommen waren.

Femme en pleurs pendant la guerre d'indépendance chypriote, Kontemenos, 16 juin 1958. Ce jour-là se déroulaient les funérailles de cinq Chypriotes grecs tués au cours d'une attaque menée par les nationalistes.

'The White Man's Burden.' A photograph taken during a night raid by British soldiers and the Kenya police to find members of the Mau Mau, 29 November 1952. The Mau Mau were members of the Kikuyu tribe who were dedicated to driving the British from their country.

„Die Bürde des weißen Mannes." Eine nächtliche Razzia britischer Soldaten und kenianischer Polizisten auf der Suche nach Mitgliedern des Mau-Mau-Geheimbundes, 29. November 1952. Die Mau-Mau, die zum Stamm der Kikuyu gehörten, wollten die britischen Kolonialherren vertreiben.

« Le fardeau de l'homme blanc. » Ce cliché fut pris lors d'un raid nocturne mené par les soldats britanniques et la police kenyane pour retrouver des Mau-Mau, 29 novembre 1952. Les Mau-Mau faisaient partie de la tribu des Kikuyu et se battaient pour le départ des Britanniques.

Police examine suspects, Kenya, November 1952. They were looking for the scars on the body that marked the seven initiation cuts for recruits to the Mau Mau.

Polizisten untersuchen verdächtige Keniaer auf Initiationsnarben, November 1952. Jeder junge Mau-Mau trug sieben Schnitte am Körper, die ihnen beim Aufnahmeritual in die Mau-Mau zugefügt werden.

Contrôle de police, Kenya, novembre 1952. Les policiers vérifiaient si ces hommes portaient sur le corps les marques de sept entailles, signes du rite d'initiation des recrues des Mau-Mau.

On 29 October 1956, Israeli forces advanced into the Sinai peninsula. When this picture was taken, four days later, they were poised to recapture Gaza.

Am 29. Oktober 1956 drangen israelische Streitkräfte bis zur Sinai-Halbinsel vor. Als vier Tage später diese Aufnahme entstand, waren sie bereit, den Gaza-Streifen zurückzuerobern.

Avancée des troupes israéliennes dans le Sinaï, 29 octobre 1956. Ce cliché fut pris quatre jours plus tard, alors qu'elles étaient sur le point de reconquérir Gaza.

Israeli troops interrogate peasants in Gaza, 19 November 1956. The Israeli
Foreign Minister, Golda Meir, had justified seizure of the Gaza strip as an integral
part of Israel, 'for the good of the inhabitants and their neighbours outside it'.

Israelische Soldaten verhören ortsansässige Bauern im Gaza-Streifen,
19. November 1956. Die israelische Außenministerin Golda Meir hatte die
Besetzung des Gaza-Streifens zur Integration in das israelische Staatsgebiet damit
gerechtfertigt, daß sie „zum Wohle der dortigen Einwohner und der ausländischen
Nachbarn sei".

Des soldats israéliens interrogent des paysans à Gaza, 19 novembre 1956. Mme le
ministre d'Israël des Affaires étrangères, Golda Meir, avait justifié l'occupation de
la bande de Gaza comme faisant partie intégrale d'Israël « pour le bien de ses
habitants et de leurs voisins à l'extérieur du territoire ».

The British Empire stands firm, for a few more days at least. A sentry guards British HQ in Ishmailia during the Suez Crisis of 1956. Beside him is an Egyptian who has come to register a complaint. A great many complaints were registered against the British at that time.

Das Britische Weltreich bleibt standfest, zumindest noch einige Tage lang. Ein Wachtposten patrouilliert vor dem britischen Hauptquartier in Ismailija während der Suez-Krise von 1956. Zu jener Zeit wurden zahlreiche Beschwerden gegen die Briten vorgebracht.

L'Empire britannique ne vacille pas, du moins pas encore. Sentinelle montant la garde au quartier général britannique d'Ishmailia pendant la crise de Suez de 1956. A côté de lui se tient un Egyptien venu déposer une plainte. A cette époque, de nombreuses plaintes furent déposées contre les Britanniques.

A distraught Arab
woman approaches
a British post in Port
Saïd after her house
has been destroyed
by bombing,
8 November 1956.

Eine verzweifelte
Araberin nähert sich
einem britischen
Posten in Port Said,
nachdem ihr Haus
durch Bomben
zerstört worden ist,
8. November 1956.

Détresse d'une
femme arabe qui se
dirige vers un poste
britannique à Port
Saïd après la
destruction de sa
maison durant un
bombardement,
8 novembre 1956.

Egyptian children prepare for trouble in October 1956, just a few days before the invasion. After President Nasser seized the Suez Canal in July, war was not inevitable, but colonial attitudes on the part of the British and French governments made it highly likely.

Wenige Tage vor der Invasion bereiten sich ägyptische Kinder auf die bevorstehenden Unruhen vor, Oktober 1956. Nachdem Präsident Nasser im Juli den Suezkanal verstaatlicht hatte, war ein Krieg zwar nicht unvermeidbar, jedoch angesichts der kolonialistischen Einstellung der britischen wie auch der französischen Regierung sehr wahrscheinlich.

Des enfants égyptiens se préparent à la guerre quelques jours avant l'invasion, octobre 1956. La nationalisation du canal de Suez par Nasser en juillet ne devait pas aboutir à la guerre mais les gouvernements britannique et français adoptèrent une attitude très coloniale qui la rendit imminente.

British commandos raise the White Ensign over Navy House, Port Said, 8 November 1956. Might was on the side of the Europeans, right on the side of the Egyptians.

Soldaten eines britischen Kommandotrupps hissen die Fahne der Königlichen Marine über Navy House in Port Said, 8. November 1956. Die Macht lag zwar bei den Europäern, doch das Recht bei den Ägyptern.

Un commando britannique hisse le pavillon de la marine de guerre au-dessus de la Maison de la marine, Port Saïd, 8 novembre 1956. La force était du côté des Européens, le droit du côté des Egyptiens.

A crowd of anti-war protesters in Trafalgar Square at the height of the Suez Crisis, November 1956. As far as the British government was concerned, the fighting in Egypt went splendidly, but the public reaction at home was appalling.

Kriegsgegner protestieren auf dem Höhepunkt der Suez-Krise auf dem Trafalgar Square, November 1956. Die Regierung war zwar der Meinung, daß sich der Krieg in Ägypten ausgezeichnet entwickele, die britische Öffentlichkeit reagierte jedoch mit Entsetzen.

Une foule de manifestants opposés à la guerre, à Trafalgar Square, au plus fort de la crise de Suez, novembre 1956. Pour le gouvernement britannique, les combats menés en Egypte se déroulaient on ne peut mieux mais la réaction des Britanniques fut épuvantable.

Anthony Eden (hand to brow), prime minister of Britain, at the Conservative Party Conference in Llandudno, 22 October 1956. A few days later, Eden had sanctioned the attack on Egypt. Two months later he resigned. The Suez Crisis had broken him.

Der britische Premierminister Anthony Eden (mit der Hand an der Stirn) auf der Parteikonferenz der Konservativen in Llandudno, 22. Oktober 1956. Wenige Tage später gab Eden seine Zustimmung zum Angriff auf Ägypten. Zwei Monate danach legte er sein Amt nieder. Die Suez-Krise hatte ihn gebrochen.

Anthony Eden (la main au front), Premier ministre britannique, lors de la conférence du parti conservateur à Llandudno, 22 octobre 1956. Quelques jours plus tard, Eden approuvait l'attaque menée contre l'Egypte. Deux mois plus tard, il démissionnait. La crise de Suez mit un terme à sa carrière.

Russian T34 tanks clear the streets of East Berlin, 18 June 1953. The previous day, the East German government had announced increased quotas for construction workers. 50,000 protesters burnt the Red Flag and attacked the Soviet Embassy. But, as in Hungary, the tanks proved unbeatable.

Russische T34-Panzer räumen die Straßen Ost-Berlins, 18. Juni 1953. Einen Tag zuvor hatte die DDR-Regierung eine Erhöhung der Arbeitsnormen für Bauarbeiter bekanntgegeben. 50.000 Demonstranten verbrannten daraufhin die Rote Fahne und griffen die sowjetische Botschaft an. Die russischen Panzer erwiesen sich allerdings, wie schon in Ungarn, als unschlagbar.

Des chars russes T34 dégagent les rues de Berlin-Est, 18 juin 1953. La veille, le gouvernement est-allemand avait annoncé une augmentation des quotas de production pour les ouvriers du bâtiment. 50 000 manifestants brûlèrent le drapeau rouge et attaquèrent l'ambassade soviétique. Mais, comme en Hongrie, les chars furent les plus forts.

'…Meanwhile, in Hungary…' Two Hungarian freedom fighters walk past the remains of members of the AVH, the hated Hungarian secret police, 12 November 1956. The scene is outside AVH headquarters, two weeks after the rebellion broke out.

„…Unterdessen in Ungarn…" Zwei ungarische Freiheitskämpfer passieren die Leichname von Mitgliedern der AVH, der gehaßten ungarischen Geheimpolizei, 12. November 1956. Die Szene spielt sich vor dem Präsidium der AVH ab, zwei Wochen nachdem der Aufstand ausgebrochen war.

« … Pendant ce temps, en Hongrie … » Deux combattants hongrois pour la liberté passent devant les corps des policiers de l'AVH, la redoutable police secrète hongroise, 12 novembre 1956. La scène se déroule à l'extérieur du quartier général de l'AVH, deux semaines après le début du soulèvement.

A 15-year-old Hungarian with machine gun prepares to take on the Soviet invaders during the uprising in Budapest, October 1956.

Während des Aufstands in Budapest bereitet sich eine 15jährige Ungarin darauf vor, die sowjetischen Invasoren mit einem Maschinengewehr zu empfangen, Oktober 1956.

Une Hongroise de 15 ans, armée d'une mitrailleuse, prête à s'opposer à l'envahisseur soviétique durant le soulèvement, Budapest, octobre 1956.

Hungarians burn a
portrait of Stalin,
12 November 1956,
but the Soviet tanks
were already on
their way.

Ungarische Bürger
verbrennen am 12.
November 1956 ein
Porträt Stalins, die
russischen Panzer
waren jedoch schon
unterwegs.

Des Hongrois
brûlent le portrait de
Staline mais les chars
soviétiques étaient
déjà en route,
12 novembre 1956.

The heady, early
days of the rising.
Young Hungarians
with their national
flag in Budapest,
27 October 1956.

Die berauschenden
ersten Tage des
Aufstands. Junge
Ungarn schwenken
stolz ihre National-
flagge in Budapest,
27. Oktober 1956.

Les premiers jours
enivrants du mou-
vement insurrec-
tionnel. De jeunes
Hongrois avec le
drapeau national
à Budapest,
27 octobre 1956.

Western journalists witness the summary executions of members of the AVH in Budapest, November 1956. 'The secret police lie twisted in the gutter,' wrote an eye-witness, '…The Hungarians will not touch the corpse of an AVH man, not even to close the eyes or straighten a neck.'

Westeuropäische Journalisten werden in Budapest Zeuge der Hinrichtungen von Mitgliedern der AVH, November 1956. „Die Geheimpolizisten liegen verrenkt in der Gosse," schrieb ein Augenzeuge, „…Die Ungarn weigern sich, den Leichnam eines AVH-Mannes zu berühren, und sei es auch nur, um seine Augen zu schließen oder einen abgewinkelten Kopf zu richten."

Des journalistes occidentaux assistent à l'exécution sommaire d'agents de l'AVH à Budapest, novembre 1956. « Les agents de la police secrète gisent dans le caniveau », écrivit un témoin, « … Les Hongrois refusent de toucher le cadavre d'un homme de l'AVH, de lui fermer les yeux ou de lui redresser la tête ».

A member of the AVH is marched away by patriots,
November 1956. The first shots in the uprising were fired by
the AVH. From that moment, they were shown no mercy.

Ein Mitglied der AVH wird von zwei Patrioten abgeführt,
November 1956. Die ersten Schüsse, die während des Auf-
stands fielen, gab die AVH ab. Von da an hatte man kein
Erbarmen mit ihr.

Un agent de l'AVH est emmené par des patriotes, novembre
1956. Les premières balles furent tirées par l'AVH. A partir
de ce moment-là, elle fut traitée sans merci.

3. Living with the bomb
Leben mit der Bombe
Vivre avec la bombe atomique

Practical advice on how to deal with a sneak nuclear attack, 1955:
'Duck into the nearest doorway, close your eyes very tightly and try to
cover any exposed parts of the body.'

Praktischer Ratschlag für den Fall eines überraschenden Atom-
waffenangriffs, 1955: „Kauern Sie sich in den nächsten Hauseingang,
schließen Sie ganz fest die Augen, und versuchen Sie, alle unbe-
kleideten Körperteile zu bedecken."

Conseils pratiques en cas d'attaque nucléaire surprise, 1955:
« Blotissez-vous dans l'embrasure de la porte la plus proche, fermez les
yeux très fort et couvrez toutes les parties exposées de votre corps ».

3. Living with the bomb
Leben mit der Bombe
Vivre avec la bombe atomique

'The bomb' was the H-bomb. France and Britain were proud and arrogant possessors of this weapon of mass destruction, hideously more powerful than the bombs that had wiped out Hiroshima and Nagasaki. But the big players were the United States and the Soviet Union, and it was their bulging nuclear muscles and mutual distrust that fuelled the Cold War.

The bomb spawned a plethora of activity. The Campaign for Nuclear Disarmament and other anti-nuclear groups across the world marched and demonstrated. Dissent was quieter in Moscow. Spies in uniform flew to and fro in reconnaissance planes. Spies in plain clothes slipped across frontiers or fled from embassies to take up new lives in the rival camp. For a while, spy mania gripped Britain and the United States. An ill-written message on a placard brandished outside the White House during the trial of the Rosenbergs revealed popular American opinion: 'Kill all traitors. Rid the US of rats'.

False promises and ludicrous advice were offered to their own citizens by those that loved the bomb. All that was needed to save oneself from the bomb's sickly fallout was a paper bag or a bucket, a plastic sack or double-glazing.

A few believed the lies. Most simply tried to ignore the bomb and hoped it would go away.

Mit „der Bombe" meinte man die Wasserstoffbombe. Frankreich und Großbritannien waren stolze Besitzer dieser Massenvernichtungswaffe, deren Zerstörungskraft die Bomben von Hiroshima und Nagasaki, noch weit übertraf. Die eigentlichen Kontrahenten jener Zeit waren die Vereinigten Staaten und die Sowjetunion. Ihr stetig anwachsendes Waffenarsenal und das tiefe gegenseitige Mißtrauen nährte den Kalten Krieg.

Die Bombe initiierte zahlreiche Aktivitäten. Mitglieder der Kampagne für Atomare Abrüstung und andere organisierte Atomgegner demonstrierten weltweit. In Moskau äußerte sich der Widerstand zurückhaltender. Uniformierte Spione wurden auf Aufklärungsflüge geschickt. Spione in Zivil entkamen über die Grenze oder flohen über Botschaften, um im gegnerischen Lager ein neues Leben zu beginnen. Eine Zeitlang ergriff Großbritannien und die Vereinigten Staaten eine regelrechte Spionagemanie. Das Transparent, das während des Gerichtsprozesses gegen die Rosenbergs vor dem Weißen Haus hing, spiegelte die damalige Stimmung der Amerikaner wider: „Tötet alle Verräter. Befreit die Vereinigten Staaten von den Ratten."

Die Befürworter der Bombe beschwichtigten die Bürger mit falschen Versprechungen und grotesken Ratschlägen: Um sich vor dem radioaktiven Niederschlag zu schützen, sei eine Papiertüte, ein Eimer, ein Plastiksack oder doppelt verglaste Fenster ausreichend.

Wenige glaubten diese Lügen. Die meisten versuchten, die Bombe zu ignorieren, und hofften, es würde sie bald nicht mehr geben.

« La bombe «, c'était la bombe H. La France et la Grande-Bretagne étaient fières de détenir cette arme de destruction massive, d'une puissance plus terrifiante encore que celle des bombes d'Hiroshima et de Nagasaki. Mais les grands maîtres du jeu les Etats-Unis et l'Union soviétique alimentaient la guerre froide avec leur arsenal nucléaire bien garni et leur méfiance mutuelle.

La bombe atomique engendra une foule d'activités. Les militants de la Campagne pour le désarmement nucléaire, ainsi que d'autres mouvements anti-nucléaires, manifestèrent partout dans le monde, sauf à Moscou où la dissidence était plus discrète. Des espions en uniforme volaient à bord d'avions de reconnaissance tandis que des espions en civil franchissaient les frontières ou s'enfuyaient des ambassades pour commencer une nouvelle vie dans le camp adverse. La Grande-Bretagne et les Etats-Unis furent alors saisis d'espionnite. Une pancarte brandie devant la Maison Blanche pendant le procès des Rosenberg traduit bien l'opinion populaire américaine : « Exécutons les traîtres, chassons la vermine hors des Etats-Unis ».

Les défenseurs de la bombe atomique donnaient à leurs citoyens des conseils aussi invraisemblables que faux. A les en croire, en cas d'attaque nucléaire, un sac en papier, un seau, un sac en plastique ou un double vitrage pouvaient offrir une protection suffisante.

Peu de gens crurent ces mensonges. La plupart évitaient tout simplement de penser à la bombe atomique en espérant qu'elle disparaîtrait un jour.

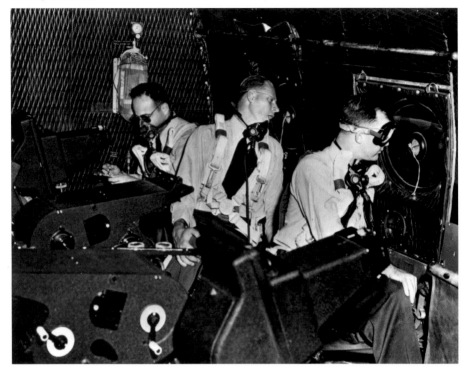

March 1953. Volunteers from the US Air Force observe atomic bursts over Nevada through specially designed windows of a transport aircraft. This was part of a test to determine the effect on the eyes. In the foreground are flash-blindness recorders.

März 1953. Freiwillige der amerikanischen Luftwaffe verfolgen durch speziell hierfür entwickelte Fenster Atomexplosionen in der Wüste Nevadas. Diese Übung war Teil eines Versuchs, die Auswirkung einer Atomexplosion auf die Augen zu bestimmen. Die Geräte im Vordergrund dienten dabei der Feststellung von Blitz-Blindheit.

Mars 1953. Des volontaires de l'armée de l'air américaine à bord d'un avion observent des explosions atomiques à travers des hublots spécialement conçus à Nevada. Cet essai devait permettre de mesurer les effets des explosions sur les yeux. Au premier plan, des appareils enregistrent les flashs éblouissants.

US Marines study an A-bomb test at Yugga Flat, Nevada, 1952. All nuclear powers used troops as guinea pigs in this fashion.

Amerikanische Marinesoldaten beobachten einen Atombombentest in Yugga Flat, Nevada, 1952. Alle Nuklearmächte benutzten auf ähnliche Weise Soldaten als Versuchskaninchen.

Des Marines américains assistent à un essai de la bombe atomique à Yugga Flat, Nevada, 1952. Toutes les puissances nucléaires utilisèrent leurs soldats comme cobayes.

The world's first nuclear-powered submarine, USS *Nautilus*, enters New York Harbour, May 1956. Two years later the *Nautilus* made the first ever voyage under the ice cap of the North Pole.

Das erste atomgetriebene U-Boot der Welt, die USS *Nautilus*, läuft in den New Yorker Hafen ein, Mai 1956. Zwei Jahre später unternahm die *Nautilus* als erstes U-Boot eine Reise unter die Eisdecke des Nordpols.

Le premier sous-marin nucléaire du monde, le USS *Nautilus*, entre dans le port de New York, mai 1956. Deux ans plus tard, le *Nautilus* effectuait le premier voyage sous la calotte glacière du pôle Nord.

Mock destruction. This test house was built in Nevada, to observe the effects of an atomic explosion. The picture was taken by a camera shooting 24 frames a second, in a lead case 60ft from the house. The source of light was the flash from the bomb itself.

Zerstörungsprobe. An diesem Testhaus in der Wüste Nevadas wurde die Wirkung einer Atomexplosion beobachtet. Eine Kamera, die 24 Bilder pro Sekunde aufnahm, befand sich 20 Meter vom Haus entfernt in einem Bleigehäuse. Als Lichtquelle für die Fotos diente der Blitz der Bombe.

Destruction simulée. Immeuble construit au Nevada pour observer l'impact d'explosions atomiques. Ce cliché fut pris avec un appareil de 24 poses/seconde posé dans une boîte en plomb placée à 20 mètres de distance. La source de lumière était le flash de la bombe.

Model destruction. The commandant of the Civil Defence
Training Centre in Quebec demonstrates the effect of an atomic
bomb bursting over his city, April 1952.

Zerstörungsmodell. Der Kommandant des Trainingszentrums
für Zivilen Bevölkerungsschutz in Quebec demonstriert die
Wirkung einer Atombombenexplosion über seiner Stadt,
April 1952.

Destruction miniature. Le commandant du Centre
d'entraînement de la défense civile de Québec explique les
conséquences d'une explosion atomique sur sa ville, avril 1952.

6 April 1958. Some of the 4,000 members of CND who marched from Trafalgar Square to the Atomic Weapons Research Establishment at Aldermaston, near Reading. Among the founders of the two-month-old CND were Bertrand Russell, Canon Collins, Michael Foot and J B Priestley.

6. April 1958. 4.000 Anhänger der CND (Campaign for Nuclear Disarmament) zogen vom Londoner Trafalgar Square zum Atomwaffen-Forschungszentrum in Aldermaston, in der Nähe von Reading. Zu den Initiatoren der erst zwei Monate alten CND gehörten Bertrand Russell, Canon Collins, Michael Foot und J. B. Priestley.

6 avril 1958. 4 000 manifestants de la CND défilaient de Trafalgar Square au Centre de recherche pour l'armement nucléaire à Aldermaston, près de Reading. Créée deux mois plus tôt, la CND comptait parmi ses fondateurs Bertrand Russell, Canon Collins, Michael Foot et J. B. Priestley.

A vast crowd of CND members and supporters at a rally in Trafalgar Square after the march from Aldermaston to London, Easter 1959. The aims of the Campaign for Nuclear Disarmament were 'to reduce the nuclear peril and to stop the armaments race, if need be by unilateral action.'

Eine enorme Menschenmenge von Anhängern der CND versammelt sich nach dem Protestmarsch 1959 von Aldermaston nach London am Trafalgar Square, Ostern 1959. Das erklärte Ziel der Protestbewegung war, „die atomare Gefahr zu reduzieren und das Wettrüsten zu beenden, falls notwendig auch durch einseitiges Handeln".

Une immense foule de militants de la CND et de sympathisants, rassemblée à Trafalgar Square, après avoir marché d'Aldermaston à Londres, Pâques 1959. La Campagne pour le désarmement nucléaire avait pour but « de réduire le danger nucléaire et de mettre fin à la course aux armements; si nécessaire, au moyen d'actions unilatérales ».

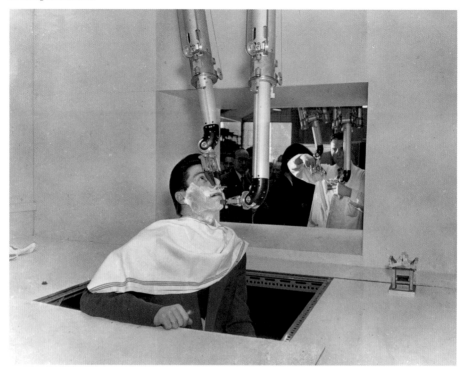

A remote-control handling apparatus is used to shave a man at a nuclear research establishment, March 1957. This was part of a publicity initiative to reassure the public of the precision of instruments used in the nuclear industry.

Ein Mann läßt sich in einem Atomforschungszentrum per Fernbedienung rasieren, März 1957. Diese Vorführung gehörte zu einer Werbekampagne, die die Öffentlichkeit beruhigen sollte, was die Präzision der in der Atomindustrie verwendeten Instrumente betraf.

Cet homme est rasé à l'aide d'un appareil télécommandé utilisé dans un centre de recherches nucléaires, mars 1957. Ce cliché faisait partie d'une campagne destinée à rassurer le public sur la précision des instruments employés dans l'industrie nucléaire.

A student on the Ford Nuclear Reactor Project disposes of radioactive waste in a lead-lined dustbin at the University of Michigan, 1955.

Ein Student der Universität von Michigan, der an einem von der Firma Ford finanzierten Kernreaktorprojekt mitarbeitet, entsorgt radioaktiven Müll in einer mit Blei ausgekleideten Abfalltonne, 1955.

Un étudiant, participant au projet de réacteur nucléaire Ford, verse des déchets radioactifs dans une poubelle plombée, Université du Michigan, 1955.

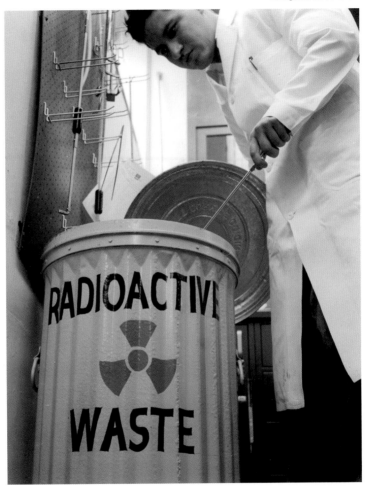

Julius and Ethel Rosenberg (born Ethel Greenglass) in a marshal's van heading for the Federal House of Detention after they had been convicted of 'wartime' espionage in 1951. Both professed their innocence, but they were executed two years later.

Julius und Ethel Rosenberg (geborene Greenglass) auf dem Weg ins bundesstaatliche Gefängnis nach ihrer Verurteilung wegen Spionage zu „Kriegszeiten", 1951. Beide beteuerten ihre Unschuld, sie wurden jedoch zwei Jahre später hingerichtet.

Julius et Ethel Rosenberg (née Ethel Greenglass) dans le fourgon de police les conduisant à la prison fédérale après leur condamnation pour espionnage en « temps de guerre », 1951. Tous deux clamèrent leur innocence mais furent exécutés deux ans plus tard.

The Third Man. Kim Philby (far right) at a press conference in London, 1955. Philby was a double agent, a communist employed by the British as head of their anti-Communist counter-espionage. He defected to the Soviet Union in 1963.

Der dritte Mann. Kim Philby (ganz rechts) bei einer Pressekonferenz in London, 1955. Philby war Doppelagent. Der Kommunist, der für die Briten als Leiter der anti-kommunistischen Gegenspionage arbeitete, setzte sich 1963 in die Sowjetunion ab.

Le troisième homme. Kim Philby (à l'extrême droite) lors d'une conférence de presse à Londres, 1955. Philby était un agent double, c'est-à-dire un communiste employé par les Britanniques comme responsable du contre-espionnage anti-communiste. Il passa à l'Union soviétique en 1963.

4. Black and white
Schwarz und Weiß
Noirs et Blancs

Far from the days of Carnival. Police search a black youth during the race riots in Notting Hill, London, September 1958. Race hatred in Britain was fuelled by ignorance, poverty and a dirty handful of politicians.

Jenseits des Karnevals. Während der Rassenunruhen von Notting Hill durchsuchen Londoner Polizisten einen Schwarzen, September 1958. Unwissenheit, Armut und rassistische Parolen einiger Politiker nährten zu jener Zeit den Rassenhaß in Großbritannien.

Eloigné du carnaval. Un policier fouille un jeune Noir durant les émeutes raciales de Notting Hill, Londres, septembre 1958. En Grande-Bretagne, la haine raciale fut alimentée par l'ignorance, la pauvreté et quelques politiciens malhonnêtes.

4. Black and white
Schwarz und Weiß
Noirs et Blancs

The Fifties were the make-or-break decade in terms of the compatibility of blacks and whites in at least three continents. In the United States, the initiative was taken by a cross-section of black society that ran from Martin Luther King to Rosa Parks, seeking to move out of the ghettos. In South Africa, the initiative came from the whites, seeking to push the black population further and further into the shanty towns.

In Britain, neither whites nor blacks had any clear agenda. Most whites were, generally speaking, unmoved; most blacks were, generally speaking, content. So it was left to the racist minority to set the tone. For those that were prepared to listen, there was plenty of good advice to be had. In 1956, Martin Luther King made some suggestions for black people seeking to assert their rights: 'If cursed, do not curse back. If pushed, do not push back. If struck, do not strike back, but evidence love and goodwill at all times.'

In the US and in Britain, progress was made in bringing black and white together. In South Africa, a long struggle lay ahead.

In mindestens drei Kontinenten prägten die fünfziger Jahre das künftige Zusammenleben von Schwarzen und Weißen. In den Vereinigten Staaten versuchten Angehörige unterschiedlichster Schichten der schwarzen Gesellschaft, von Martin Luther King bis Rosa Parks, die Farbigen zum Verlassen der Ghettos zu ermutigen. In Südafrika hingegen drängten die Weißen die schwarze Bevölkerung immer weiter in die Slums der Vorstädte ab.

In Großbritannien hatten weder die Weißen noch die Schwarzen klar strukturierte Vorstellungen. Die meisten Weißen standen der Rassenfrage im großen und ganzen gleichgültig gegenüber; die meisten Schwarzen waren im großen und ganzen zufrieden. So überließ man es einer rassistischen Minderheit, den Ton zu bestimmen. Den Meinungslosen erteilte man gute Ratschläge. Im Jahre 1956 riet Martin Luther King den Schwarzen, die ihre

Rechte behaupten wollten, folgendes: „Wenn man euch beschimpft, schimpft nicht zurück. Wenn man euch stößt, stoßt nicht zurück. Wenn man euch schlägt, schlagt nicht zurück, sondern beweist jederzeit Liebe und guten Willen."

In den Vereinigten Staaten und in Großbritannien erzielte man erste Fortschritte in der Zusammenführung von Schwarz und Weiß. In Südafrika jedoch stand beiden Seiten noch ein langer Kampf bevor.

Les années cinquante furent une décennie déterminante pour les relations entre Noirs et Blancs sur au moins trois continents. Aux Etats-Unis, une petite frange de la communauté noire, de Martin Luther King à Rosa Parks, décida de sortir du ghetto, tandis qu'en Afrique du Sud, la communauté blanche entreprit de retrancher les Noirs toujours plus à l'intérieur des bidonvilles.

En Grande-Bretagne, Blancs et Noirs n'exprimaient aucune revendication particulière. Les Blancs se sentaient, dans l'ensemble, peu concernés et les Noirs s'estimaient, dans l'ensemble, satisfaits. C'est ainsi qu'une minorité raciste put occuper le terrain et donner le ton. Quant à ceux qui étaient prêts à entendre un discours neuf, les bons conseils ne manquaient pas. En 1956, Martin Luther King adressa quelques recommandations aux Noirs qui voulaient revendiquer leurs droits : « Ne répondez pas à l'injure par l'injure. Si vous êtez bousculé, ne bousculez pas en retour. Si vous êtes frappé, ne frappez pas à votre tour. Faites preuve d'amour et de compréhension quoi qu'il arrive. »

Aux Etats-Unis et en Grande-Bretagne, un rapprochement entre les deux communautés s'opéra. En Afrique du Sud, la lutte serait très longue encore.

West Indian immigrants arrive at Victoria
Station, London, July 1959. They were near
the end of a journey by boat and train that
had taken several days, but they still had to
find work, and somewhere to live.

Westindische Einwanderer bei ihrer Ankunft
am Victoria-Bahnhof, London, Juli 1959. Die
mehrtägige Schiffs- und Eisenbahnreise
hatten sie hinter sich. Jetzt mußten sie noch
Arbeit und eine Unterkunft finden.

Arrivée d'immigrés antillais à Victoria Station,
Londres, juillet 1959. Ils étaient presque au
bout d'un voyage de plusieurs jours par bateau
et train. Il leur restait maintenant à trouver du
travail et un endroit pour vivre.

June 1956.
Haywood Magee's
portrait of
immigrants at
Southampton
Docks, just after
their arrival
in Britain.

Juni 1956. Diese
Aufnahme von
Haywood Magee
zeigt Einwanderer
bei ihrer Ankunft
im Hafen von
Southampton in
Großbritannien.

Juin 1956.
Haywood Magee a
photographié ces
immigrantes au port
de Southampton, à
leur arrivée en
Grande-Bretagne.

Some of the first arrivals from Jamaica at home in Brixton, south
London, December 1952. At that time, the law neither permitted nor
outlawed racism in Britain, but there was a distinct danger that a
'colour bar' was springing up.

Einige der ersten Ankömmlinge aus Jamaika in Brixton, Süd-London,
Dezember 1952. Zu jener Zeit gab es in Großbritannien keinerlei
Gesetze, die den Rassismus gestatteten oder untersagten. Die Gefahr,
daß sich eine „Rassenschranke" bildete, wurde jedoch immer größer.

L'une des premières familles jamaïcaines installées à Brixton, au sud de
Londres, décembre 1952. A cette époque, il n'y avait aucune loi en
Grande-Bretagne pour permettre ou condamner le racisme mais le
danger de voir émerger une « ségrégation raciale » était bien réel.

Sign of the times:
'Rooms to let – No
coloured men'.
By 1958 the attitude
of many whites was
hardening.

Ein Zeichen der
Zeit: „Zimmer zu
vermieten – Nicht
an Farbige". Bis
1958 hatte sich die
Einstellung vieler
Weißer verhärtet.

Signe des temps:
« Chambres à
louer – Interdit
aux gens de cou-
leur ». En 1958,
l'attitude d'un grand
nombre de Blancs
s'était durcie.

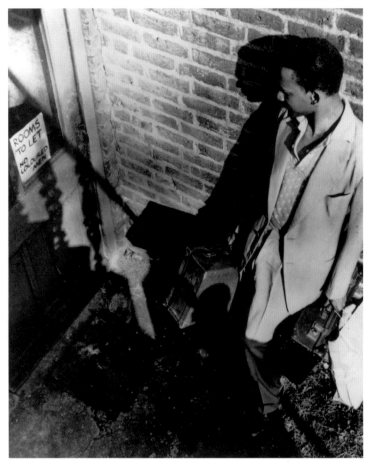

Blenheim Crescent, Notting Hill, London,
2 September 1958. Trouble had flared on
24 August, when five black men were beaten
by white youths. Over the next two weeks it
escalated. On the day this picture was taken,
2,000 white youths attacked black houses.

Blenheim Crescent, Notting Hill,
2. September 1958. Nachdem am 24. August
weiße Jugendliche fünf Schwarze
zusammengeschlagen hatten, brachen
Unruhen aus. In den folgenden zwei Wochen
spitzte sich die Lage zu. Als diese Aufnahme
entstand, stürmten 2.000 weiße Jugendliche
Häuser, in denen Schwarze wohnten.

Blenheim Crescent, Notting Hill, Londres,
2 septembre 1958. Un premier incident éclata
le 24 août quand cinq Noirs furent battus par
de jeunes Blancs. Au cours des deux semaines
suivantes, la tension ne fit que monter. Le
jour où ce cliché fut pris, 2 000 jeunes Blancs
attaquèrent les maisons où vivaient des Noirs.

An enormous capacity to hate. Members of the Ku Klux Klan (KKK)
choose the unlikely setting of the Pleasure Gardens, Battersea Park,
London for a poorly attended torchlit rally during the Festival of
Britain, 6 October 1951.

Grenzenloser Haß. Mitglieder des Ku-Klux-Klans wählen über-
raschenderweise die Szenerie der Pleasure Gardens im Londoner
Battersea Park für einen Fackelzug, der wenig Interesse fand, während
des Festival of Britain, 6. Oktober 1951.

Une énorme capacité à haïr. Les membres du Ku Klux Klan (KKK)
choisissent le décor invraisemblable du Pleasure Gardens, Battersea
Park, à Londres pour une manifestation peu suivie lors du Festival de
Grande-Bretagne, le 6 octobre 1951.

March 1959.
Members of the
White Defence
League assemble in
Trafalgar Square
to whip up hatred
against black
immigrants.

März 1959. An-
hänger des Weißen
Verteidigungsbundes
versammeln sich auf
dem Trafalgar
Square, um den
Haß gegen schwarze
Einwanderer zu
schüren.

Mars 1959.
Militants de la
Ligue de défense
des Blancs réunis
à Trafalgar Square
pour attiser la haine
envers les immigrés
noirs.

Too stupid to be a joke, too evil to be taken lightly. The sign by the roadside in Johannesburg, South Africa, proclaims apartheid paranoia. There were many such signs to be seen in 1956, when this picture was taken by Ejor.

Zu dumm, um als Witz zu gelten, und zu übel, um auf die leichte Schulter genommen zu werden. Ein Straßenschild in Johannesburg warnt vor den schwarzen Einwohnern. Als Ejor im Jahre 1956 dieses Bild aufnahm, gab es viele derartige öffentliche Hinweise.

Trop stupide pour être une blague, trop méchant pour être pris à la légère. Ce panneau au bord d'une route à Johannesbourg révèle la paranoïa de l'apartheid. Il était fréquent de voir de telles enseignes en 1956, date à laquelle Ejor prit ce cliché.

September 1957. A racist student is persuaded to leave the campus by Federal troops, Little Rock Central High School, Arkansas. It took 1,000 soldiers and 10,000 National Guardsmen to force desegregation on the school.

September 1957. Bundessoldaten zwingen einen rassistischen Studenten, das Schulgelände zu verlassen, Little-Rock-Oberschule, Arkansas. 1.000 Soldaten und 10.000 Nationalgardisten waren im Einsatz, um an dieser Schule gemischtrassigen Unterricht durchzuführen.

Septembre 1957. Des soldats de l'armée fédérale obligent un étudiant raciste à quitter le campus du lycée central de Little Rock, Arkansas. Il fallut le renfort de 1 000 soldats et de 10 000 gardes nationaux pour instaurer la déségrégation dans l'école.

The writing on the wall – a Notting Hill street, 1959. The graffiti reads,
'No colour bar here – yet'. The number of black immigrants arriving in
Britain each year by then exceeded 50,000.

Schriftzug an einer Mauer – in einer Straße in Notting Hill, 1959. Das
Graffiti besagt: „Keine Rassenschranke hier – noch nicht". Damals
wanderten jährlich über 50.000 Schwarze nach Großbritannien ein.

Signe des temps au mur – dans une rue de Notting Hill, 1959. Le graffiti
dit « Pas de ségrégation ici – pour l'instant ». A cette époque, plus de
50 000 immigrés noirs arrivaient en Grande-Bretagne chaque année.

Looking to the future. Guests at a Christmas party at Holland Park Comprehensive School, London, December 1958. The party had been organized by recent immigrants to Britain for children from many ethnic backgrounds.

Blick in die Zukunft. Eine Weihnachtsfeier in der Gesamtschule in Holland Park, Dezember 1958. Einwanderer, die erst vor kurzem nach Großbritannien gekommen waren, organisierten diese Feier für Kinder unterschiedlicher Nationalitäten.

Tournés vers le futur. Enfants à la fête de Noël de l'école de Holland Park, Londres, décembre 1958. La fête avait été organisée par des immigrés récemment établis en Angleterre pour les enfants d'origines diverses.

5. Work
Arbeit
Le travail

July 1958. A milkman feeds one of the newly installed parking meters in Mayfair, London. These were the first meters in the capital. You may wonder why a milk delivery service should have to pay for parking – was the milkman really that slow, or was he delivering milk to a large block of flats?

Juli 1958. Ein Milchmann wirft im Londoner Stadtteil Mayfair eine Münze in eine der ersten Parkuhren der Metropole. Bleibt nur die Frage, weshalb ein Milchmann für die Zustellung eine Parkgebühr bezahlte – war er tatsächlich so langsam oder lieferte er die Milch zu einem großen Wohnkomplex?

Juillet 1958. Un laitier met une pièce dans un parcomètre fraîchement installé à Mayfair, Londres. C'était l'un des premiers parcomètres de la capitale. On peut se demander pourquoi le laitier devait lui aussi payer sa place de parking – était-il si lent ou livrait-il du lait dans un arrondissement?

5. Work
Arbeit
Le travail

Work was as unpalatable in the Fifties as it had always been, but at least there was plenty of it. The world swung into full-time post-war production, and miners and steelworkers, shipwrights and factory hands, sweated to provide a hungry public with all the necessities and luxuries of life. Work was unpleasant, hours were still long – in many cases people worked a five-and-a-half-day week. There were closed shops and demarcation disputes, for trade unions still had enough members and enough clout to challenge employers. There were plenty of strikes.

As yet there was not a computer in sight, and vast office rooms were filled with clerks attending to mountains of dockets and invoices. Good spelling and good handwriting were marketable skills. A job was for life. No one thought of early retirement. No one thought of being headhunted.

There were plenty of apprenticeships for talented young men, and plenty of mind-numbing jobs for young girls and older women. Equal pay was still a far-off dream. Average pay was $25 a week in the United States. To the rest of the world, that seemed like good money.

Arbeit behagte den Menschen in den fünfziger Jahren zwar ebensowenig wie zu anderen Zeiten, aber wenigstens konnte man sich über einen Mangel an ihr nicht beklagen. Die Welt stürzte sich auf die Nachkriegsproduktion, und Bergarbeiter wie Stahlarbeiter, Schiffbauer wie Fabrikarbeiter schufteten, um den Bedarf an allen notwendigen Dingen und Luxusgütern zu stillen. Die Arbeitsbedingungen waren nicht gerade angenehm und die Arbeitszeiten noch immer lang; vielerorts arbeitete man fünfeinhalb Tage die Woche. Die Gewerkschaften hatten damals noch ausreichend Mitglieder und genügend Schlagkraft, um den Arbeitgebern die Stirn zu bieten. Streiks waren an der Tagesordnung.

Das Computerzeitalter war noch nicht eingeläutet, und ein Heer von Angestellten arbeitete in riesigen Büroräumen Berge von Laufzetteln und Rechnungen ab. Gute Rechtschreibkenntnisse und eine saubere Handschrift waren Fähigkeiten, die Marktwert besaßen. Wer eine Anstellung hatte, behielt sie sein Leben lang. Niemand dachte an vorzeitige Pensionierung oder daran, sich abwerben zu lassen.

Es gab Lehrstellen im Überfluß für talentierte junge Männer und stumpfsinnige Tätigkeiten für junge Mädchen und ältere Frauen. Gleiche Bezahlung für Männer und Frauen war damals noch ein unerreichbarer Traum. Das durchschnittliche Einkommen betrug in den Vereinigten Staaten 25 $ pro Woche. Dem Rest der Welt schien das eine Menge Geld.

S'il était aussi déplaisant de travailler dans les années cinquante que par le passé, au moins y avait-il du travail en abondance. Le monde de l'après-guerre entrait dans une ère de production à plein régime. Mineurs, sidérurgistes, ouvriers des chantiers navals et des usines, tous travaillaient durement pour fournir aux consommateurs affamés les biens et articles de luxe qu'ils réclamaient. Le travail était pénible et les heures longues – dans bien des cas, les gens avaient encore des semaines de cinq jours et demi. Les arrêts de travail et les conflits étaient fréquents, les syndicats comptant encore assez d'adhérents et étant assez puissants pour défier les employeurs. Il y eut de nombreuses grèves.

A cette époque, on ne connaissait pas encore les ordinateurs : d'immenses bureaux étaient remplis d'employés, affairés à établir des fiches et des factures. Une bonne orthographe et une belle écriture étaient, par conséquent, des qualités fort prisées sur le marché. On gardait son emploi à vie. Personne ne songeait à la retraite anticipée ou aux chasseurs de tête.

Une foule d'apprentissages s'offraient à la disposition des jeunes gens doués et une foule d'emplois stupides à celle des jeunes filles et des femmes plus âgées. L'égalité des salaires n'était encore qu'un lointain rêve. Aux Etats-Unis, le salaire moyen s'élevait à 25 $ par semaine. Pour le reste du monde, c'était beaucoup d'argent.

The back-room boys. Military clerks in the Pentagon, Washington, processing personnel files of fellow members of the United States Army, 1950. As usual, it was a busy decade for US troops.

Die Experten im Hintergrund. Militärische Verwaltungsangestellte bearbeiten in Washington im Pentagon die Personalakten ihrer Kameraden in der Armee, 1950. Wie immer, gab es auch in diesem Jahrzehnt für US-Soldaten viel zu tun.

Des experts en coulisse. Employés militaires du Pentagone affectés au traitement des dossiers personnels de leurs collègues, Washington, 1950. Les soldats américains eurent fort à faire au cours de cette décennie, comme toujours.

December 1954. Haywood Magee's picture of some of the workforce employed by Littlewood's Pools. This was a Saturday, so they were probably dealing with incoming coupons, forecasting the results of that day's football matches.

Dezember 1954. Haywood Magees Aufnahme zeigt Angestellte der Toto-Wettgesellschaft Littlewood's. Es war ein Samstag, wahrscheinlich bearbeiteten sie die letzten noch eintreffenden Totoscheine, die die Fußballergebnisse jenes Spieltages betrafen.

Décembre 1954. Cliché de Haywood Magee montrant le personnel de la société de pari Littlewood au travail. C'était un samedi, les employés traitaient probablement les fiches de pari concernant les résultats des matchs de football du jour.

December 1958. Rushing to meet the Christmas demand. A worker selects a pair of eyes for a doll at the Lines Brothers factory, Morden, South London. Lines Brothers were one of the most prestigious toymakers in Britain, also making Hornby trains and Meccano sets.

Dezember 1958. Das Weihnachtsgeschäft läuft auf Hochtouren. Eine Arbeiterin der Gebrüder-Lines-Fabrik wählt Augen für eine Puppe aus, Morden, Süd-London. Die Lines Brothers gehörten zu den renommiertesten Spielzeugfabrikanten Großbritanniens. Sie stellten auch die Hornby-Eisenbahnen und Meccano-Bausätze her.

Décembre 1958. Satisfaire les commandes de Noël. Une ouvrière choisit une paire d'yeux pour une poupée à l'usine des Lines Brothers, à Morden au sud de Londres. C'était le fabricant de jouets le plus prestigieux de Grande-Bretagne. Il produisait, entre autres, les trains Hornby et les jeux de Meccano.

The largest steel beam ever rolled in Europe, April 1958. It was made by Dorman Long and Co at their mill in Lackenby, North Yorkshire.

Die größten Stahlträger, die je zuvor in Europa produziert wurden, April 1958. Sie wurden im Stahlwalzwerk von Dorman Long and Co. in Lackenby, Nord-Yorkshire, hergestellt.

La plus grande poutre en acier jamais fabriquée en Europe, avril 1958. C'était l'œuvre de Dorman Long and Co. dans leur aciérie de Lackenby, au nord du Yorkshire.

A London bus conductor at work, 1955. By the mid-Fifties, public
transport in London relied heavily on immigrants from the Caribbean.

Ein Schaffner bei der Arbeit in einem Londoner Bus, 1955. Mitte der
fünfziger Jahre waren die öffentlichen Verkehrsmittel in hohem Maße
auf die Arbeitskraft von Einwanderern aus der Karibik angewiesen.

Un contrôleur de bus londonien au travail, 1955. Au milieu des
années cinquante, les transports en commun londoniens
dépendaient pour beaucoup des immigrés venus des Caraïbes pour
assurer le service.

February 1954. Workers in Tilbury, near London, use their electric polishers to put the final touches to the deck of the P&O liner *Arcadia*, before the ship's maiden voyage to Australia.

Februar 1954. Reinigungskräfte in Tilbury, bei London bringen mit Hilfe modernster Geräte das Deck des P&O Passagierschiffs *Arcadia* vor seiner Jungfernfahrt nach Australien auf Hochglanz.

Février 1954. Des employés à Tilbury, près de Londres, polissent une dernière fois le pont du paquebot de la P&O, l'*Arcadia* avec des cireuses électriques, avant son voyage inaugural à destination de l'Australie.

Bert Hardy's picture of one of 20,000 enumerators at work on a traffic census in Britain, September 1954. In those days the traffic flow was still sufficiently small to keep a tally with pencil and paper.

Diese Aufnahme von Bert Hardy zeigt einen der 20.000 Helfer einer in Großbritannien durchgeführten Verkehrszählung, September 1954. In jenen Tagen war es noch möglich, die Anzahl der Fahrzeuge mit Papier und Bleistift zu bewältigen.

Cliché de Bert Hardy – l'une des 20 000 personnes recrutées pour le recensement de la circulation en Grande-Bretagne, septembre 1954. A cette époque, le trafic n'était pas très dense et il était encore possible de pointer les voitures au crayon sur une feuille de papier.

The cutting edge of Fifties technology. Operators dealing with 999 Emergency calls to the police in the new Information Room at Scotland Yard, London, December 1956.

Allerneueste Technologie der fünfziger Jahre. Vermittler nehmen im neuen Informationsraum von Scotland Yard, London, Notrufe unter 999 entgegen, Dezember 1956.

Technologie de pointe dans les années cinquante. Employés traitant les appels d'urgence adressés au 999 de la police dans le nouveau service de renseignements de Scotland Yard, Londres, décembre 1956.

The interior of a large Marks and Spencer store, November 1955.
At the time, there were many who decried the modern shopping culture for
having sacrificed personal service on the altar of efficiency.

Eine riesige Verkaufshalle von Marks and Spencer, November 1955. Viele
Kunden klagten darüber, daß sie in der modernen, anonymen Konsumwelt
zugunsten höherer Effizienz auf eine persönliche Beratung verzichten mußten.

A l'intérieur d'un grand magasin Marks and Spencer, novembre 1955. A cette
époque, un grand nombre de gens dénoncèrent ce nouveau type de commerce
au nom duquel le service individuel était sacrifié sur l'autel de l'efficacité.

Self-service replaces the personal touch. Louise Simonson helps herself at a supermarket in Connecticut, USA, 1950.

Selbstbedienung ersetzt das individuelle Verkaufsgespräch. Louise Simonson beim Einkauf in einem Supermarkt in Connecticut, USA, 1950.

Le self-service remplace le service individuel. Louise Simonson se sert elle-même dans un supermarché du Connecticut, Etats-Unis, 1950.

Personal service was still readily available in the Fifties. The original caption read: 'Only a man equipped with extraordinary powers of patience and endurance is fitted to this task.'

Der persönliche Service war in den fünfziger Jahren dennoch weit verbreitet. Die ursprüngliche Bildunterschrift lautete: „Nur ein Mann, der mit außergewöhnlicher Geduld und Ausdauer gesegnet ist, eignet sich für diese Aufgabe."

Dans les années cinquante, le service individuel était néanmoins encore très répandu. La légende d'origine était la suivante : « Seul un homme armé d'une patience et d'une résistance hors du commun peut accomplir ce travail ».

Exhausted shop assistants relax at the end of a hard day's work. 'Sales' were as popular in the Fifties as they are today.

Erschöpfte Verkäuferinnen nach einem harten Arbeitstag. „Schlußverkäufe" waren in den fünfziger Jahren ebenso beliebt wie heutzutage.

Détente pour des vendeuses épuisées après une dure journée de travail. Les « soldes » étaient aussi populaires dans les années cinquante qu'elles le sont aujourd'hui.

6. Leisure
Freizeit
Les loisirs

July 1951. One of photographer Bert Hardy's most famous pictures, taken on the promenade at Blackpool with a fixed-focus box camera. Nearly 50 years later it was still being used on travel posters in Britain.

Juli 1951. Eine der berühmtesten Fotografien von Bert Hardy, aufgenommen an der Strandpromenade von Blackpool mit einer Fixfocus-Boxkamera. Noch knapp 50 Jahre später diente sie in Großbritannien als Motiv für Plakate mit Reisewerbung.

Juillet 1951. L'une des plus célèbres photographies de Bert Hardy, prise sur la promenade de Blackpool avec un appareil à angle fixe. Près de 50 ans plus tard, on peut encore voir en Grande-Bretagne des affiches de voyage avec cette image.

6. Leisure
   Freizeit
   Les loisirs

Few people in the Fifties had television to entertain them at home. Not many had cars to whisk them away for an outing from home. On the other hand, most provincial towns still had a theatre and a resident company of actors. People sang in pubs and village halls, or gathered round the piano in the parlour. At Easter and Whitsun there might be a visit from a travelling fair or circus.

Sunday was sacred, a time when the shops were closed and the factories silent. But there was little enough to do on this one day of leisure in the week. The cinema opened late, the pubs closed early. There was no racing, no football, no sport of any kind. A walk by the canal in winter or an excursion by train to the sea in summer was all that beckoned.

But horizons were widening. The jumbo jet had arrived, opening up the possibilities of a cheap week's holiday hundreds of miles away, in resorts that had seemed impossibly remote and exotic. For those who couldn't afford such luxury, there were plenty of holiday camps; 10 years earlier, the chalets they stayed in may well have housed soldiers or airmen, or even prisoners of war.

Kaum jemand besaß in den fünfziger Jahren einen Fernseher, der daheim für Unterhaltung sorgte, und nur wenige hatten Autos, die Abwechslung auf einem Ausflug versprachen. Dafür gab es in den meisten Provinzstädten jedoch ein Theater und eine ortsansässige Schauspieltruppe. Die Menschen sangen in Lokalen und Gemeindehallen oder scharten sich um ein Klavier im Salon. Zu den Oster- oder Pfingstfeiertagen besuchte mitunter ein Zirkus oder ein Jahrmarkt die Stadt.

Der Sonntag war heilig – die Geschäfte blieben geschlossen, und der Fabriklärm verstummte. Doch an diesem einen Tag in der Woche, den man der Muße widmen konnte, gab es kaum Freizeitmöglichkeiten. Die Kinovorstellungen begannen spät, und die Lokale schlossen früh. Es gab keine Rennen, keine Fußballspiele, überhaupt keine Sport-veranstaltungen. Ein Spaziergang am Kanal im Winter oder ein Ausflug ans Meer mit der Eisenbahn im Sommer waren die einzigen Verlockungen.

Doch der Horizont begann, sich zu erweitern. Die Jumbojets ermöglichten einen Pauschalurlaub Hunderte von Kilometern entfernt, in Ferienzielen, die früher unerreichbar weit und exotisch schienen. Wer sich solchen Luxus nicht leisten konnte, reiste in Feriendörfer, deren Apartments 10 Jahre zuvor Soldaten, Fliegern oder sogar Kriegsgefangenen als Unterkunft gedient haben mochten.

Dans les années cinquante peu de gens possédaient un poste de télévision pour se distraire à la maison ou une voiture pour s'évader dans la nature le temps d'une balade. Par contre, presque toutes les villes de province disposaient encore d'un théâtre et d'une compagnie permanente. Les gens avaient coutume de chanter dans les pubs et les salles communales ou de se réunir au salon autour d'un piano. A Pâques et à la Pentecôte, il était fréquent d'avoir la visite d'une foire ambulante ou d'un cirque.

Le dimanche était sacré. Les magasins étaient fermés et les usines silencieuses. Il n'y avait pas grand-chose à faire durant cet unique jour de repos de la semaine. Le cinéma commençait tard, les pubs fermaient tôt. Il n'y avait ni course, ni match de football, ni aucun autre événement sportif. Tout au plus pouvait-on envisager une promenade au bord du canal en hiver et, en été, une excursion en train au bord de la mer.

Mais de nouveaux horizons s'ouvraient. Le jumbo-jet venait de naître, offrant la possibilité de passer des vacances bon marché à des milliers de kilomètres de chez soi en des lieux qui, jusque-là, semblaient inaccessibles et exotiques. Quant à ceux qui n'en avaient pas les moyens, il existait toutes sortes de camps de vacances, notamment dans des chalets qui, 10 ans plus tôt, avaient hébergé des soldats, des pilotes et même des prisonniers de guerre.

June 1952. Two girls enjoy the thrill of 'the
Looper' at the newly re-opened Pleasure
Gardens, Battersea Park, London.

Juni 1952. Nervenkitzel für die beiden
Mädchen auf dem „Looper" im kürzlich
wiedereröffneten Pleasure Gardens, Battersea
Park, London.

Juin 1952. Quelques frissons pour deux
jeunes filles sur « the Looper » au parc
d'attraction Pleasure Gardens récemment
réouvert dans Battersea Park à Londres.

Bert Hardy's photograph of off-duty cabaret dancers having fun at a fairground stall in Margate on the Kent coast. For some young people, jobs away from home gave them their first taste of freedom.

Revuetänzerinnen, außerhalb des Kaberetts fotografiert von Bert Hardy, amüsieren sich an einem Jahrmarktstand in Margate an der Küste von Kent. Ein Job weit von zu Hause entfernt gab einigen jungen Leuten den ersten Geschmack auf Freiheit.

Danseuses de cabaret photographiées par Bert Hardy, lors de l'une de leurs virées aux stands forains à Margate sur la côte du Kent. Le travail loin de chez soi offrait un premier goût de liberté à certains jeunes gens.

July 1953. Holidaymakers sunbathe outside their chalets at Butlin's Holiday Camp, Filey, Yorkshire. It seems that Bert Hardy spent much of every summer touring Britain on behalf of the *Picture Post* magazine, in which these pictures first appeared.

Juli 1953. Feriengäste sonnen sich vor ihren Apartments in Butlin's Feriendorf, Filey, Yorkshire. Bert Hardy bereiste offenbar jeden Sommer Großbritannien im Auftrag der Zeitschrift *Picture Post*, in der diese Bilder erstmals erschienen.

Juillet 1953. Bain de soleil pour ces vacancières devant leur petit chalet au Butlin's Holiday Camp, Filey, Yorkshire. Il semblerait que Bert Hardy passait l'essentiel de ses étés à faire le tour de la Grande-Bretagne pour le compte du magazine *Picture Post* qui publia ces clichés pour la première fois.

Off-duty cancan, 1959. Dancers from London's Pigalle Club provide Fifties titillation on the caterpillar ride at the Battersea Festival Gardens. The picture was taken on the gala opening day of the funfair.

Ein Cancan außerhalb der Arbeitszeiten, 1959. Tänzerinnen des Londoner Nachtclubs Pigalle bei einer Fahrt auf der Raupe in den Festival Gardens von Battersea. Diese Aufnahme entstand am Eröffnungstag des Rummelplatzes.

French cancan en dehors des heures de travail, 1959. Ces danseuses du Pigalle Club de Londres savent émoustiller le public sur les montagnes russes du festival de Battersea. Ce cliché fut pris le jour de l'inauguration de la foire.

A Bert Hardy
picture of
sunbathers on a
Piccadilly rooftop in
the heart of London,
July 1953.

Diese Sonnenan-
beterinnen im
Herzen Londons
porträtierte Bert
Hardy auf einem
Dach in Piccadilly,
Juli 1953.

Bain de soleil sur
un toit de Piccadilly
au cœur de Londres,
juillet 1953, cliché
de Bert Hardy.

May 1956.
Lunchtime visitors
crowd the terrace at
the Oasis Swimming
Pool, Holborn,
London.

Mai 1956. Zur
Mittagszeit Hoch-
betrieb auf der
Sonnenterrasse des
Schwimmbades
Oasis, Holborn,
London.

Mai 1956. La ter-
rasse de la piscine de
l'Oasis envahie à
l'heure du déjeuner,
Holborn, Londres.

Blackpool Tower, July 1953. Three friends cram into an automatic photographic booth called 'the Photomaton'. For once *Picture Post* had sent a different photographer to cover a seaside story – Ronald Startup.

Blackpool Tower, Juli 1953. Drei Freunde drängen sich in einen Fotoautomaten, den sogenannten „Photomaton". Diesmal hatte die *Picture Post* einen anderen Fotografen geschickt, um in einem Seebad eine Fotoreportage zu machen, nämlich Ronald Startup.

Tour de Blackpool, juillet 1953. Trois amis, entassés dans une cabine de photographie automatique appelée « photomaton ». Pour une fois, le *Picture Post* avait envoyé un autre photographe, Ronald Startup, pour réaliser un reportage au bord de la mer.

A Lambeth couple scan the paper to decide which film to see on their night out in London's West End, 1955. They have exactly one pound to spend. The film on the poster – *Ain't Misbehavin'* – was billed as a lively American version of *Pygmalion*.

Ein Paar aus Lambeth studiert in der Tageszeitung die Filme, die am Abend im West End, London, gezeigt werden, 1955. Ihr Vergnügen darf nicht mehr als ein englisches Pfund kosten. Der Film *Ain't Misbehavin'* wurde als eine amerikanische Version des Theaterstücks *Pygmalion* angekündigt.

Un couple de Lambeth regarde dans le journal quel film aller voir le soir de leur sortie dans le West End, Londres, 1955. Ils ont exactement une livre Sterling en poche. Le film à l'affiche – *Ain't Misbehavin'* – était annoncé comme une adaptation américaine très animée de *Pygmalion*.

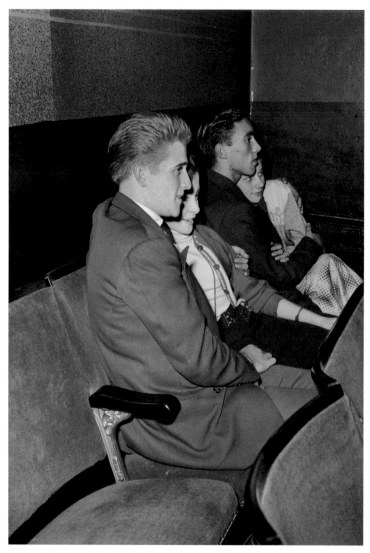

Inside the Western
Talkie Theatre
in Bradford, 1955.
The theatre had
special 'couples'
chairs', with no
central arm rest.

Das Western Talkie
Theatre in Bradford,
1955. Zur Aus-
stattung dieses Kinos
zählten besondere
Sitzreihen für Paare
ohne störende Arm-
lehnen.

A l'intérieur du
Western Talkie
Theatre de
Bradford, 1955. Ce
cinéma avait des
sièges spécialement
conçus pour les
couples, sans
accoudoir au milieu.

Highgate, London 1955. A debutante and her beau at a coming-out ball for the British actress Anna Massey. This was the year of her theatrical debut as Jane in *The Reluctant Debutante*.

Highgate, London, 1955. Eine Debütantin und ihr attraktiver Begleiter auf einem Ball zu Ehren der britischen Schauspielerin Anna Massey, die in jenem Jahr ihren ersten Auftritt am Theater hatte. Sie spielte die Rolle der Jane in dem Stück *The Reluctant Debutante*.

Highgate, Londres, 1955. Une débutante et son prétendant lors du bal donné pour l'actrice britannique Anna Massey. Cette année-là, elle fit ses débuts au théâtre dans le rôle de Jane, pour *The Reluctant Debutante*.

Kurt Hutton's picture of the interior of the Mocamba, Knightsbridge, August 1954. It was one of dozens of coffee bars that opened in London during the mid-Fifties, serving Italian-style coffee with a good head of froth in glass cups and saucers.

Diese Fotografie des Interieurs des Mocamba, Knightsbridge, nahm Kurt Hutton auf, August 1954. Das Mocamba war eines der vielen Cafés, die Mitte der fünfziger Jahre in London eröffnet wurden und in dem man den beliebten italienischen Cappuccino in Gläsern servierte.

Cliché de Kurt Hutton – à l'intérieur du Mocamba, Knightsbridge, août 1954. Ce café, comme les dizaines d'autres ouverts à Londres au milieu des années cinquante, servait dans des verres du café à la mode italienne avec de la mousse qui débordait partout.

7. Entertainment
Unterhaltung
Divertissements

Miles Davis and Jeanne Moreau, 1957. In the Fifties, Davis worked
with Gil Evans, producing a series of albums that were melodic and
colourful. Moreau starred in a number of French New Wave films,
portraying sensual and world-weary characters.

Miles Davis und Jeanne Moreau, 1957. In den fünfziger Jahren
arbeitete Davis gemeinsam mit Gil Evans und nahm eine Reihe von
melodischen und vielseitigen Schallplatten auf. Moreau spielte
Hauptrollen in zahlreichen französischen Filmen der Nouvelle Vague
und verkörperte mit Vorliebe sinnliche und der Welt überdrüssige
Figuren.

Miles Davis et Jeanne Moreau, 1957. Dans les années cinquante,
Davis travailla avec Gil Evans. Ils produisirent une série d'albums aux
sons mélodieux et colorés. Moreau apparut dans de nombreux films
français de la Nouvelle Vague, incarnant des personnages à la fois
sensuels et las du monde.

7. Entertainment
   Unterhaltung
   Divertissements

Some of the shine left the tinsel of Hollywood as the golden days of the studio system came to an end. But as Tinseltown declined, other centres of film production prospered. In Sweden, Ingmar Bergman produced three of his masterpieces: *The Seventh Seal*, *Wild Strawberries* and *The Face*. François Truffaut and Jean-Luc Godard rewrote the scenario for French film, and the Italian Federico Fellini won two Oscars – for *La Strada* and *Le Notte di Cabiria*.

Musically, jazz moved smoothly from Bebop to Cool. The big bands of Basie, Ellington, Herman and Goodman kept on swinging. Then all hell broke loose when Bill Haley and the Comets released a number called *Rock Around the Clock*. Now it seems mild enough. At the time it was held responsible for every sin from sex to socialism.

There was revolution in the theatre. John Osborne's *Look Back in Anger* was seen at the time as a play that dealt a mortal blow to old-style drama. It was an uncomfortable piece, taut and unfriendly, with a new theatrical phenomenon – the anti-hero.

Millions still listened to the radio, but, in the darkened corners of many a room, little boxes spluttered and hissed and glowed with silvery light. The Television Age was upon us.

Als die goldene Ära des Studiosystems zu Ende ging, verlor zwar Hollywood ein wenig von seinem Glanz, doch nun begann man endlich, auch Notiz von anderen Zentren der Filmproduktion zu nehmen. In Schweden drehte Ingmar Bergman drei seiner Meisterwerke: *Das siebente Siegel*, *Wilde Erdbeeren* und *Das Gesicht*. François Truffaut und Jean-Luc Godard revolutionierten den französischen Film, und der Italiener Federico Fellini errang zwei Oscars – für *Das Lied der Straße* und *Die Nächte der Cabiria*.

In der Musikszene entwickelte sich der Jazz vom Bebop zum Cool Jazz, während die Big-Band-Orchester von Count Basie, Duke Ellington, Woody Herman und Benny Goodman sich weiterhin dem Swing verpflichteten. Doch plötzlich entfesselten Bill Haley und die Comets mit ihrem Stück *Rock Around the Clock* einen Orkan. Aus heutiger Sicht war es eine vergleichsweise harmlose Musik. Damals aber machte man sie für jede Sünde und alles Schlechte verantwortlich, das man sich vorstellen konnte – vom Sex bis zum Sozialismus.

Auch im Theater vollzog sich eine Revolution: Zeitgenössischen Kritikern zufolge versetzte John Osbornes Drama *Blick zurück im Zorn* dem althergebrachten Theater einen Todesstoß. Es war ein unbequemes Stück, das eine angespannte, unfreundliche Atmosphäre auf die Bühne brachte und ein neues dramatisches Phänomen präsentierte – den Antihelden.

Noch immer lauschten Millionen von Menschen dem Radio. Doch vielerorts, in abgedunkelten Ecken, zischten bereits ominöse kleine Kästen mit flimmerndem Licht. Das Zeitalter des Fernsehens hatte begonnen.

Les meilleurs quittèrent le monde doré de Hollywood quand sonna le glas de la grande époque des studios. Mais, tandis que Hollywood déclinait, de nouvelles capitales du cinéma florissaient. En Suède, Ingmar Bergman tourna trois chefs-d'œuvre : *Le septième sceau*, *Les fraises sauvages* et *Le visage*. En France, François Truffaut et Jean-Luc Godard revolutionnaient le cinéma tandis que l'Italien Federico Fellini était récompensé par deux Oscars – pour *La Strada* et *Les Nuits de Cabiria*.

En musique, le jazz évoluait peu à peu du bebop vers le cool jazz; les grands orchestres de Basie, Ellington, Herman et Goodman étaient toujours aussi entraînants. Mais la sortie de l'album *Rock Around the Clock* de Bill Haley and the Comets fit l'effet d'une bombe. Aujourd'hui, on le trouverait plutôt inoffensif tandis qu'à l'époque, on lui attribua tous les péchés de la terre, du sexe jusqu'au communisme.

Au théâtre, c'était la révolution. *La Paix du dimanche* de John Osborne fut considérée comme la pièce qui porta un coup décisif au théâtre traditionnel. Son climat était inconfortable, tendu et inamical et, phénomène nouveau au théâtre, la pièce mettait en scène l'anti-héros.

Des millions de gens écoutaient encore la radio. Mais, dans le coin obscur de plus d'une pièce, de petites boîtes émettaient des images dans un bain de lumière argentée. L'âge de la télévision commençait.

Jayne Mansfield poses for photographs at the Dorchester Hotel, London,
September 1957. Mansfield was regarded by critics as the poor man's
Marilyn Monroe. But then, the parts Mansfield was offered in movies were
uniformly dreadful.

Jayne Mansfield bei einem Fototermin im Dorchester Hotel, London, September
1957. Kritiker sahen in ihr die Marilyn Monroe des armen Mannes. Schließlich
war von den Filmrollen, die man ihr anbot, eine so schlecht wie die andere.

Jayne Mansfield pose pour des photographes à l'hôtel Dorchester, Londres,
septembre 1957. Les critiques voyaient en Mansfield la Marylin Monroe du
pauvre. Il est vrai que les personnages incarnés par Mansfield étaient
tous misérables.

July 1958. 'Big' Joe Turner, the American jazz singer and pianist, taking pictures at the Cannes Jazz Festival. An expert in the hard-driving 'stride' piano style, Turner was known as the 'Boss of the Blues'. Like many American musicians, he settled permanently in France in the Fifities.

Juli 1958. Der amerikanische Jazzsänger und Pianist „Big" Joe Turner nimmt beim Jazz-festival in Cannes Fotos auf. Turners Spezialität am Klavier war der „Stride"-Pianostil. Man nannte ihn den „Boß des Blues", und wie viele amerikanische Musiker verlegte er in den fünfziger Jahren seinen Wohnsitz nach Frankreich.

Juillet 1958. Le « grand » Joe Turner, chanteur et pianiste américain de jazz, prend des photos au festival de jazz de Cannes. Surnommé « le maître du blues », il maîtrisait parfaitement au piano le style « stride », issu du Ragtime. Comme beaucoup d'autres musiciens américains, il s'installa définitivement en France dans les années cinquante.

Diana Dors (left) and Ginger Rogers at the Cannes Film Festival in 1956. In Dors, the British film industry believed it had at last produced a Hollywood-style blonde sex symbol. Rogers's career was in a trough. She was described by one producer as 'smiling and grinning and unreal'.

Diana Dors (links) und Ginger Rogers beim Filmfestival in Cannes, 1956. In Diana Dors glaubte die britische Filmindustrie, endlich ein blondes Sexsymbol im Stile Hollywoods hervorgebracht zu haben. Die Karriere von Ginger Rogers war hingegen auf einem Tiefpunkt angelangt. Ein Produzent beschrieb sie als „lächelnd, grinsend und unwirklich".

Diana Dors (à gauche) et Ginger Rogers au festival de Cannes en 1956. Avec Dors, le cinéma britannique espérait avoir enfin trouvé son sex-symbol blond dans le style de Hollywood. La carrière de Rogers était en perte de vitesse. Selon un producteur, elle « souriait, grimaçait et semblait irréelle ».

July 1956. Marilyn Monroe and her husband, playwright Arthur Miller, outside their rented home at Englefield Green near London, Miller wrote of Monroe: 'with all her radiance she was surrounded by a darkness'.

Juli 1956. Marilyn Monroe und ihr Ehemann, der Dramatiker Arthur Miller, in Englefield Green bei London. Miller schrieb über seine Frau: „Trotz ihrer strahlenden Erscheinung war sie von Dunkelheit umgeben".

Juillet 1956. Marilyn Monroe et son mari, le dramaturge Arthur Miller, devant leur maison louée à Englefield Green, près de Londres. Miller écrivit à son sujet : « Malgré tout son éclat, elle semblait entourée d'obscurité ».

October 1950. Montgomery Clift and Irene Dunne arrive at London Airport. They were to attend the Command Performance of *The Mudlark*.

Oktober 1950. Montgomery Clift und Irene Dunne bei ihrer Ankunft auf dem Londoner Flughafen. Sie besuchten die königliche Galavorstellung von *The Mudlark*.

Octobre 1950. Montgomery Clift et Irene Dunne à leur arrivée à l'aéroport de Londres. Ils étaient venus assister à la première du film *The Mudlark*, en présence de la reine.

Audrey Hepburn and Fred Astaire in Paris, July 1956. They were on location filming scenes for the Gershwin musical *Funny Face*. The film crew had problems controlling the French crowds, so they dressed some of the extras as policemen.

Audrey Hepburn und Fred Astaire in Paris, Juli 1956. Sie hielten sich dort zu Dreharbeiten für das Gershwin-Musical *Funny Face* auf. Als die Filmleute die französischen Fans nicht länger in Schach halten konnten, kostümierten sie kurzerhand einige der Statisten als Polizisten.

Audrey Hepburn et Fred Astaire à Paris, juillet 1956. Ils étaient venus tourner des scènes en extérieur de la comédie musicale de Gershwin *Funny Face*. L'équipe technique ayant de la peine à contenir la foule de curieux, quelques figurants se déguisèrent en policier pour leur prêter main forte.

Joan Crawford has her corsage adjusted by a friend at the Dorchester Hotel, London, 1956. The article in which this picture was to feature was never published.

Ein Freund Joan Crawfords korrigiert den Sitz ihrer Korsage im Dorchester Hotel, London, 1956. Der Artikel, in dem dieses Bild erscheinen sollte, wurde nie veröffentlicht.

Le corsage de Joan Crawford ajusté par un ami à l'hôtel Dorchester, Londres, 1956. L'article qui devait accompagner cette photographie ne fut jamais publié.

Humphrey Bogart and Katharine Hepburn in London, April 1951. It was the year in which they made their one film together – *The African Queen.*

Humphrey Bogart und Katharine Hepburn in London, April 1951. In jenem Jahr drehten sie ihren einzigen gemeinsamen Film – *The African Queen.*

Humphrey Bogart et Katharine Hepburn à Londres, avril 1951. Cette année-là, ils tournèrent le seul film où ils jouent ensemble – *La Reine africaine.*

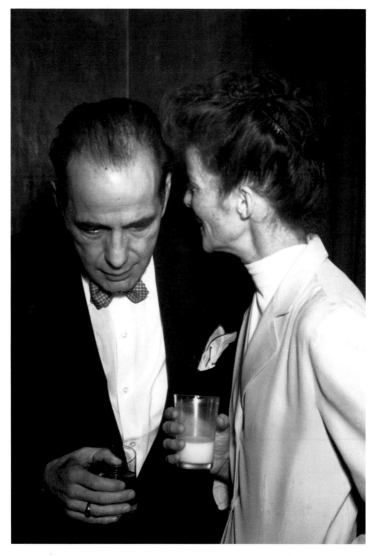

February 1953.
Vivien Leigh and
Sir Laurence Olivier
doing all they can
not to attract
attention as they
arrive at Rome
Airport.

Februar 1953.
Vivien Leigh und Sir
Laurence Olivier
geben sich auf dem
Flughafen von Rom
große Mühe, mög-
lichst unauffällig zu
erscheinen.

Février 1953.
Vivien Leigh et Sir
Laurence Olivier
font leur possible
pour ne pas attirer
l'attention à leur
arrivée à l'aéroport
de Rome.

Elizabeth Taylor in 1957, almost hidden by the pigeons of Trafalgar Square. It was the year of her marriage to Mike Todd.

Elizabeth Taylor im Jahre 1957, kaum zu erkennen inmitten der Tauben am Trafalgar Square. In jenem Jahr heiratete sie Mike Todd.

Elisabeth Taylor en 1957, presque cachée par les pigeons de Trafalgar Square. Ce fut l'année de son mariage avec Mike Todd.

The pouting sex
kitten of the Fifties,
Brigitte Bardot
in a dance studio,
February 1956.

Der berühmteste
Schmollmund der
fünfziger Jahre,
Brigitte Bardot in
einem Tanzstudio,
Februar 1956.

La moue la plus sexy
des années
cinquante Brigitte
Bardot, dans un
studio de danse,
février 1956.

July 1952. Gina
Lollobrigida in
blowsy mood. To
Americans, she was
the Italian Monroe.
To Italians, Monroe
was the American
'La Lollo'.

Juli 1952. Gina
Lollobrigida in
schlechter Verfas-
sung. Für die
Amerikaner war
sie die italienische
Monroe. Für die
Italiener war die
Monroe die ameri-
kanische „La Lollo".

Juillet 1952. Gina
Lollobrigida dans
une posture
désinvolte. Pour les
Américains, elle était
la Monroe italienne.
Pour les Italiens,
Monroe était la
« Lollo » américaine.

James Dean (left) and Corey Allen on the set of *Rebel Without a Cause* in 1955. Dean was at the height of his career – he was killed in a car crash a few months later. Allen stayed in Hollywood, and later directed *Star Trek: The Next Generation*.

James Dean (links) und Corey Allen bei Dreharbeiten zu *Denn sie wissen nicht, was sie tun*, 1955. Dean befand sich auf dem Höhepunkt seiner Karriere. Wenige Monate später kam er bei einem Autounfall ums Leben. Allen blieb in Hollywood und drehte nach seinem Wechsel ins Regiefach *Star Trek: The Next Generation*.

James Dean (à gauche) et Corey Allen sur le plateau de *La fureur de vivre* en 1955. Dean était au sommet de sa carrière. Il se tua dans un accident de voiture quelques mois plus tard. Allen resta à Hollywood et tourna plus tard *Star Trek : La nouvelle génération*.

John Huston on the set of *Moulin Rouge*, a film he directed in 1952. The first 20 minutes of the film were wonderfully photographed and edited. After that, despite all Huston's efforts, it was reckoned to be increasingly boring.

Regisseur John Huston im Jahre 1952 bei Dreharbeiten zu *Moulin Rouge*. Die ersten 20 Minuten dieses Films beeindruckten sowohl durch wunderschöne Kameraeinstellungen wie auch durch den Schnitt. Leider galt der Rest des Films als unendlich langweilig.

John Huston sur le plateau de *Moulin rouge* qu'il tourna en 1952. Les 20 premières minutes du film sont superbement mises en scène et filmées. Ensuite, et malgré tous les efforts de Huston, le film devient très ennuyeux.

October 1958. Richard Burton as Jimmy Porter during the filming of a scene from *Look Back in Anger* at Chris Barber's Jazz Club, London.

Oktober 1958. Richard Burton als Jimmy Porter während der Dreharbeiten zu einer Szene aus *Blick zurück im Zorn*, die in Chris Barbers Londoner Jazz Club aufgenommen wurde.

Octobre 1958. Richard Burton dans le rôle de Jimmy Porter pendant le tournage d'une scène de *La Paix du dimanche* au Chris Barber's Jazz Club, Londres.

Marlon Brando at a press conference in Paris, 1950. He was there to promote his latest film, Fred Zinnemann's *The Men*.

Marlon Brando bei einer Pressekonferenz in Paris, Oktober 1958. Er warb dort für seinen neuesten Film, *Die Männer*, den er unter Fred Zinnemanns Regie gedreht hatte.

Marlon Brando lors d'une conférence de presse à Paris, 1950. Il était venu faire la promotion de son dernier film, *Les Hommes* de Fred Zinnemann.

June 1953. Three knights of the English theatre in high-kicking spirits: (left to right) Laurence Olivier, John Mills and John Gielgud. The occasion was a Midnight cabaret at the London Palladium.

Juni 1953. Drei Ritter der englischen Theaterwelt in Höchstform: (von links nach rechts) Laurence Olivier, John Mills und John Gielgud. Ihr Auftritt war Teil einer Varietévorstellung im Londoner Palladium.

Juin 1953. Trois chevaliers du théâtre anglais en grande forme : (de gauche à droite) Laurence Olivier, John Mills et John Gielgud. Ils participaient à un spectacle de cabaret au Palladium de Londres.

Mary Martin, as Ensign Nellie Forbush, leaps across the stage in the West End production of Rodgers' and Hammerstein's *South Pacific* at the Drury Lane Theatre, 1951.

Mary Martin, als Ensign Nellie Forbush, springt in der West-End-Produktion von Rogers und Hammersteins Musical *South Pacific* quer über die Bühne des Drury Lane Theatre, 1951.

Mary Martin, dans le rôle d'Ensign Nellie Forbush, bondit sur scène dans le spectacle *South Pacific* de Rodger et Hammerstein, monté au Drury Lane Theatre dans le West End, 1951.

Stan ('the Man') Kenton at a concert in Britain, March 1956. The visit by Kenton's orchestra was one of the first permitted by US and British Musicians' Unions.

Stan („the Man") Kenton bei einem Konzert in Großbritannien, März 1956. Das Gastspiel von Kentons Orchester war eines der ersten, das die amerikanischen und britischen Musikergewerkschaften gestatteten.

Stan (« the Man ») Kenton lors d'un concert en Grande-Bretagne, mars 1956. La tournée de l'orchestre de Kenton fut l'une des premières autorisées par les syndicats des musiciens américain et britannique.

June 1957. A skiffle group at full throttle on board the paddle-steamer *Royal Daffodil*, sailing from London to Calais. Skiffle was a British craze; all that was needed to form a band was a guitar, a washboard, and a bass made from a tea-chest, broom handle and parachute cord.

Juni 1957. Eine Skiffle-Gruppe an Bord des Raddampfers *Royal Daffodil*, unterwegs von London nach Calais. Der Skiffle war eine verrückte britische Mode. Alles, was man für die Gründung einer Band benötigte, war eine Gitarre, ein Waschbrett und einen Baß, den man aus einer Kiste, einem Besenstiel und einer Fallschirmleine bastelte.

Juin 1957. Un groupe de skiffle bien chauffé sur le bateau à roues *Royal Daffodil* ralliant Londres à Calais. Le skiffle faisait fureur en Grande-Bretagne. Pour jouer, il suffisait d'une guitare, d'une planche à laver et d'une basse construite avec une caisse à thé, un manche à balai et une corde de parachute.

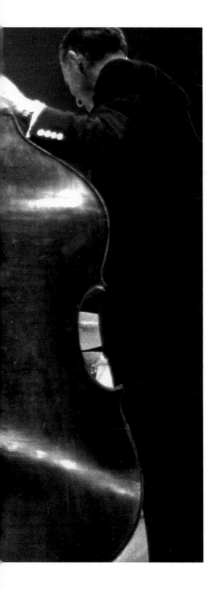

May 1956. The Louis Armstrong All Stars visit Britain: (from left to right) Edmond Hall (clarinet), Satchmo (trumpet), Trummy Young (trombone), and Arvell Shaw (bass).

Mai 1956. Die Louis Armstrong All Stars sind zu Gast in Großbritannien: (von links nach rechts) Edmond Hall (Klarinette), Satchmo (Trompete), Trummy Young (Posaune) und Arvell Shaw (Baß).

Mai 1956. Les All Stars de Louis Armstrong en tournée en Grande-Bretagne. (De gauche à droite) Edmond Hall (clarinette), Satchmo (trompette), Trummy Young (trombone) et Arvell Shaw (contrebasse).

Lady Day sings the blues, 1954. By this stage in her career Billie Holiday was addicted to drugs, but her voice was as wistful and wonderful as ever.

Lady Day singt den Blues, 1954. Zu diesem Zeitpunkt war Billie Holiday bereits drogenabhängig, doch ihre Stimme klang so schwermütig und wunderbar wie immer.

Lady Day chante le blues, 1954. A cette époque, Billie Holliday se droguait déjà mais sa voix était plus mélancolique et plus merveilleuse que jamais.

April 1957. The kid from Red Bank, NJ. Count Basie re-formed his sixteen-piece band in the mid-Fifties, made several stunning albums, and toured all over the world.

April 1957. Der Junge aus Red Bank, New Jersey. Mitte der fünfziger Jahre nahm Count Basie mit seiner erneut formierten sechzehnköpfigen Band eine Reihe großartiger Platten auf und begeisterte weltweit das Publikum auf Konzerttourneen.

Avril 1957. Au milieu des années cinquante, Count Basie, le gamin de Red Bank, New Jersey, reforma un orchestre de 16 musiciens avec lequel il produisit plusieurs albums étonnants et effectua des tournées dans le monde entier.

November 1954.
The Beverley Sisters
– (from left) Babs,
Joy and Teddie –
cluster round Irving
Berlin at the piano.

November 1954.
Die Beverley
Sisters – (von links)
Babs, Joy und
Teddie – umringen
den Komponisten
Irving Berlin.

Novembre 1954.
Les Beverley Sisters
– (à partir de la
gauche) Babs, Joy
et Teddie – réunies
au piano autour
d'Irving Berlin.

Wladziu Valentino Liberace signs the hand of one of his many admirers at London's Festival Hall, October 1954. Liberace was a brilliant entertainer, a pianist with a virtuoso style and a vulgar taste. 'Do you like my jewellery?' he would say to his audiences. 'You should do – you paid for it.'

Wladziu Valentino Liberace gibt einer seiner vielen Verehrerinnen ein Autogramm auf die Hand, Festival Hall, London, Oktober 1954. Liberace war ein brillanter Entertainer und virtuoser Pianist, allerdings mit schlechtem Geschmack. „Mögen Sie meinen Schmuck?" fragte er mitunter sein Publikum. „Das sollten Sie tun – schließlich haben Sie ihn bezahlt."

Wladziu Valentino Liberace signe un autographe sur la main de l'une de ses nombreuses admiratrices au Festival Hall, Londres, octobre 1954. Artiste de talent et pianiste virtuose, il était néanmoins vulgaire. « Aimez-vous mes bijoux ? » demandait-il au public. « J'espère que oui – c'est vous qui payez ».

Frankie Laine walks incognito through London's Leicester Square, September 1954. Laine was a Chicago-born Italian with a strong and beautiful voice. Many of his greatest hits were recorded in the Fifties: *I Believe*, *Mule Train*, *Jezebel*, *That Lucky Old Sun*, and the definitive version of *High Noon*.

Frankie Laine überquert unerkannt den Londoner Leicester Square, September 1954. Der in Chicago geborene Italiener besaß eine kraftvolle, schöne Stimme. Viele seiner größten Erfolge nahm er in den fünfziger Jahren auf: *I Believe, Mule Train, Jezebel, That Lucky Old Sun* und die maßgebliche Version von *High Noon*.

Frankie Laine incognito à Leicester Square, Londres, septembre 1954. Laine, un Italien de Chicago, avait une voix belle et puissante. La plupart de ses grands succès furent enregistrés dans les années cinquante : *I Believe, Mule Train, Jezebel, That Lucky Old Sun,* et la version définitive de *High Noon*.

April 1959. Fifteen-year-old American singing sensation Brenda Lee rehearses in a London street. She was due to appear on ITV's *Oh Boy!* – a 'big beat' television show – to promote her first hit, *Sweet Nothin's*.

April 1959. Das fünfzehnjährige amerikanische Stimmwunder Brenda Lee probt in den Straßen Londons. Sie bereitete sich auf ihren Auftritt in *Oh Boy!* vor – einer populären Fernsehshow des Senders ITV – in der sie ihren ersten Hit, *Sweet Nothin's*, vorstellen sollte.

Avril 1959. Brenda Lee, une chanteuse américaine de quinze ans qui fit sensation à l'époque, répète dans une rue de Londres. Elle devait participer à l'émission de la chaîne ITV *Oh Boy!* – un programme de télévision à grande audience – pour faire la promotion de son premier succès *Sweet Nothin's*.

The Goons in 1951 – (left to right) Peter Sellers, Spike Milligan, Michael Bentine and Harry Secombe. In the Fifties, Milligan wrote over 250 radio scripts for this brilliant and anarchic comedy team, whose success surprised and bewildered many BBC officials.

Die Goons, 1951 – (von links nach rechts) Peter Sellers, Spike Milligan, Michael Bentine und Harry Secombe. Milligan schrieb in den fünfziger Jahren über 250 Radiosendungen für dieses brillante und anarchistische Komiker-Team, dessen Erfolg in den oberen Etagen der BBC für große Überraschung und einige Verwunderung sorgte.

Les Goons, 1951 – (de gauche à droite) Peter Sellers, Spike Milligan, Michael Bentine et Harry Secombe. Dans les années cinquante, Milligan écrivit plus de 250 pièces radio-phoniques pour cette formidable et folle équipe d'humoristes dont le succès étonna et déconcerta plus d'un responsable de la BBC.

Jonathan Miller at Cambridge in 1954. Miller was one of the Beyond the Fringe quartet, with Peter Cook, Dudley Moore, and Alan Bennett. Later he became a doctor, author, and opera and theatre director.

Jonathan Miller in Cambridge im Jahre 1954. Er war eines der Mitglieder des Quartetts Beyond the Fringe um Peter Cook, Dudley Moore und Alan Bennett. Anschließend wurde er Arzt, Autor und führender Opern- und Theaterregisseur.

Jonathan Miller à Cambridge en 1954. Miller faisait partie du quartet Beyond the Fringe avec Peter Cook, Dudley Moore et Alan Bennett. Par la suite, il devint médecin, puis auteur et metteur en scène d'opéra et de théâtre.

March 1958. The British comedian Benny Hill rehearses for one of his television comedy shows at the TV Theatre, London. Hill's roguish delivery and sexist comedy style were popular in the United States and much of Europe.

März 1958. Der britische Komiker Benny Hill bei den Proben für eine seiner Fernsehshows im Londoner TV Theatre. Seine spitzbübische und sexistische Komik war in den Vereinigten Staaten und in großen Teilen Europas sehr beliebt.

Mars 1958. L'acteur britannique Benny Hill répète l'un de ses shows télévisés au TV theatre de Londres. Son style polisson et sexiste était populaire aux Etats-Unis et dans une grande partie de l'Europe.

September 1951.
Norman Wisdom in
London Melody
at the Empress Hall,
London. He is
leaping to read the
music which is
on a high stand.

September 1951.
Norman Wisdom in
London Melody
in der Empress Hall,
London. Um die
Noten lesen zu
können, muß er in
die Luft springen.

Septembre 1951.
Norman Wisdom
dans *London
Melody* saute pour
lire sa partition très
haut placée,
Empress Hall,
Londres.

British playwright and actor Peter Ustinov in 1952, making up in his dressing room for a performance of his play, *The Love of Four Colonels.*

Der britische Dramatiker und Schauspieler Peter Ustinov bereitet sich in der Theatergarderobe auf eine Vorstellung seines Stückes *Die Liebe der vier Obersten* vor, 1952.

L'acteur et dramaturge britannique Peter Ustinov se prépare dans sa loge avant de monter en scène pour jouer une de ses pièces, *The Love of Four Colonels*, 1952.

A publicity picture of the English actor Paul Schofield for *Espresso Bongo*, a 'coffee bar' musical set in Soho in the late Fifties.

Eine Werbeaufnahme mit dem englischen Schauspieler Paul Schofield für *Espresso Bongo*, ein Musical über ein Café in Soho in den späten Fünfzigern.

Une publicité avec l'acteur anglais Paul Schofield pour l'*Espresso Bongo*, un café musical ouvert à Soho à la fin des années cinquante.

The showgirls' dressing room at the Pigalle nightclub, Piccadilly, London, June 1953.

Die Garderobe der Showtänzerinnen des Nachtclubs Pigalle am Piccadilly, London, Juni 1953.

La loge des danseuses du Pigalle, un nightclub à Piccadilly, Londres, juin 1953.

Members of the famous Bluebell Troupe relax after a
rehearsal at the Nuevo Teatro in Milan, February 1952.
The Bluebell Girls were the most glamorous, if not the
most accomplished, group of dancers in Europe.

Tänzerinnen der berühmten Bluebell-Truppe nach einer
Probe im Nuevo Teatro in Mailand, Februar 1952.
Die Bluebell Girls waren damals die glamouröseste,
wenn nicht sogar die vielseitigste Tanzgruppe in Europa.

Détente pour les danseuses de la célèbre compagnie
des Bluebells après une répétition au Nuevo Teatro à
Milan, février 1952. Les Bluebell Girls étaient les
danseuses les plus éblouissantes et probablement les plus
talentueuses d'Europe.

Dancers at the Moulin Rouge nightclub in Paris, 1956. The original windmill was built in 1885, but it was converted into a dance hall in 1900. Little had changed by the Fifties: the costumes and the artistes were much the same. Only the showgirls were new and young.

Tänzerinnen im Pariser Nachtclub Moulin Rouge, 1956. Die Windmühle stammte aus dem Jahre 1885 und wurde um 1900 in einen Tanzsaal umgebaut. Bis zu den fünfziger Jahren hatten sich die Darbietungen und die Kostüme kaum verändert. Nur die Revue-Girls waren neu und jung.

Danseuses au Moulin rouge à Paris, 1956. Le moulin fut construit en 1885 puis transformé en salle de spectacles en 1900. Cinquante ans plus tard, rien ou presque n'avait changé. Les costumes et les numéros semblaient les mêmes. Seules les danseuses étaient nouvelles et jeunes.

Ginger Stanley strikes a pose worthy of Esther Williams in the mammoth water tank that provided the setting for her 'underwater ballet', 1956.

Ginger Stanley in einer Pose, die Esther Williams alle Ehre gemacht hätte. In einem gigantischen Wassertank tanzte sie ihr „Unterwasser-Ballett", 1956.

Ginger Stanley exécute un mouvement qui n'est pas sans rappeler Esther Williams dans l'énorme bassin qui fut le décor de son « ballet aquatique », 1956.

8. The Arts
Die schönen Künste
Les arts

The French abstract artist Georges Mathieu at work in his studio, June 1956. Mathieu worked on large canvasses, producing thick, heavy lines that stood in almost half relief from the surface. He called his work 'lyrical abstraction'.

Der französische abstrakte Maler Georges Mathieu in seinem Atelier, Juni 1956. Mathieu bedeckte großflächige Leinwände mit pastosen Pinselhieben, die auf der Oberfläche ein Relief bildeten, und nannte sein Werk „lyrische Abstraktion".

Le Français Georges Mathieu, peintre abstrait, à l'œuvre dans son atelier, juin 1956. Mathieu travaillait sur des grandes toiles et peignait des lignes épaisses et subtiles qui créaient un demi-relief sur la surface. C'était pour lui de l'« abstraction lyrique ».

8. The Arts
Die schönen Künste
Les arts

At first glance it would seem that it was a decade of death for the arts. Prokofiev, Sibelius, Nijinsky, Shaw, O'Neill, Charlie Parker, Rouault, Léger, Matisse and Dufy were among those who passed away – though Grandma Moses kept painting till her death, aged 101 in 1961.

Some giants still flourished: Stravinsky, Frank Lloyd Wright, Le Corbusier and Picasso. And there were plenty of 'angry young men' leaving the wings and strutting out onto centre stage: John Osborne, Jack Kerouac, Kingsley Amis, Jasper Johns, Robert Rauschenberg. Jackson Pollock arrived on the scene, cycling over many a canvas, but was killed in a car crash in 1956.

Even in the arts, Capitalism and Communism slogged away at each other. Picasso wrote a letter to the Secretary General of the French Communist Party asserting that he had not abandoned social realism. *Dr Zhivago* was published in the Fifties, but Pasternak turned down the Nobel Prize for Literature in 1958. The Moscow Young Communist League had already denounced him as 'a pig'.

And there was madness about. Ezra Pound, who had pleaded insanity to avoid being charged with treason, was released in 1958. Churchill's widow burnt Sutherland's portrait of her husband. The artist said it was 'an act of vandalism unequalled in the history of art.'

In den schönen Künsten der fünfziger Jahre dominierte auf den ersten Blick der Tod: Prokofjew, Sibelius, Nijinsky, Shaw, O'Neill, Charlie Parker, Rouault, Léger, Matisse und Dufy starben – während Grandma Moses noch bis zu ihrem Tod im Jahre 1961, 101 Jahre alt, malte.

Doch es blieben auch einige Genies: Igor Strawinsky, Frank Lloyd Wright, Le Corbusier und Pablo Picasso. Eine ganze Reihe „zorniger junger Männer" stand ebenfalls im Mittelpunkt des Interesses: John Osborne, Jack Kerouac, Kingsley Amis, Jasper Johns und

Robert Rauschenberg. Jackson Pollock fand zum Action Painting und radelte mit dem Fahrrad über viele Meter Leinwand, bis er 1956 bei einem Autounfall ums Leben kam.

Selbst vor der Kunst machte der Kampf zwischen Kapitalismus und Kommunismus nicht halt. Pablo Picasso teilte dem Generalsekretär der französischen Kommunistischen Partei schriftlich mit, daß er den Sozialistischen Realismus nicht aufgegeben habe. Boris Pasternak veröffentlichte in den fünfziger Jahren *Dr. Schiwago*. Er mußte jedoch im Jahre 1958 den Nobelpreis dafür ablehnen. Die Junge Kommunistische Liga in Moskau hatte ihn bereits als „Schwein" denunziert.

Auch der Wahnsinn brach gelegentlich durch. Ezra Pound, der auf Geisteskrankheit plädiert hatte, um einer Anklage wegen Hochverrats zu entgehen, wurde 1958 wieder entlassen. Churchills Witwe verbrannte Sutherlands Porträt ihres Gatten. Der Maler bezeichnete dies als „Vandalismus, der in der Geschichte der Kunst seinesgleichen sucht".

À première vue, cette décennie semble avoir été funeste pour le monde des arts avec la disparition de Prokofiev, Sibelius, Nijinsky, Shaw, O'Neill, Charlie Parker, Rouault, Léger, Matisse et Dufy – même si grand-mère Moses continua à peindre jusqu'à sa mort en 1961, à l'âge de 101 ans.

Il restait encore quelques géants : Stravinski, Frank Lloyd Wright, Le Corbusier et Picasso. Et, surtout, de nombreux « jeunes gens en colère » sortaient des coulisses pour occuper le devant de la scène : John Osborne, Jack Kerouac, Kingsley Amis, Jasper Johns, Robert Rauschenberg. Jackson Pollock fit son entrée et s'imposa, lui qui roulait à vélo sur ses toiles, mais fut tué dans un accident de voiture en 1956.

Les arts étaient également le théâtre de règlements de comptes entre capitalistes et communistes. Picasso adressa une lettre au Secrétaire général du parti communiste français dans laquelle il réaffirmait son soutien au réalisme socialiste. Le *Docteur Jivago*, publié dans les années cinquante, valut à Pasternak le prix Nobel de littérature de 1958 mais l'écrivain le refusa car il faisait déjà figure de traître aux yeux de la Ligue des jeunes communistes de Moscou.

L'époque semblait folle. Ezra Pound avait invoqué la folie pour ne pas être condamnée pour trahison : il fut libéré en 1958. La veuve de Churchill brûla le portrait de son mari par Sutherland. Le peintre dit que c'était là un « acte de vandalisme inégalé dans l'histoire de l'art ».

The Surrealist painter Salvador Dalí in his studio at Port Lligat, November 1951. In the background is part of his painting, *Christ of St John of the Cross*. Dalí's religious paintings of the Fifties were interspersed with more erotic work.

Der surrealistische Maler Salvador Dalí in seinem Atelier in Port Lligat, November 1951. Im Hintergrund sein Gemälde *Der Christus des heiligen Johannes vom Kreuz*. Neben den religiösen Bildern der fünfziger Jahre, malte Dalí auch erotischere Werke.

Le peintre surréaliste Salvador Dalí dans son atelier de Port Lligat, novembre 1951. A l'arrière-plan, on distingue une partie de son tableau, *Le Christ de saint Jean de la Croix*. Les peintures religieuses de Dalí, dans ces années-là, alternaient avec des œuvres plus érotiques.

Pablo Picasso with a vast carving of a goat, outside his villa 'La Californie' in Cannes, September 1955. While Franco ruled Spain, Picasso remained in exile. Dalí could not have cared less.

Pablo Picasso mit einer großen Ziegen-skulptur vor seiner Villa „La Californie" in Cannes, September 1955. Solange Franco in Spanien regierte, blieb Picasso im Exil. Dalí hingegen interessierte sich für all dies nicht.

Pablo Picasso, appuyé contre une grande sculpture de bouc devant sa villa « La Californie » à Cannes, septembre 1955. Picasso resta en exil aussi longtemps que Franco fut au pouvoir, contrairement à Dalí que cela ne préoccupa pas du tout.

The French author, critic, actor, director, painter and poet Jean Cocteau takes a ride on a carousel horse, 1950.

Der französische Autor, Kritiker, Schauspieler, Regisseur, Maler und Dichter Jean Cocteau auf einem Karussellpferd, 1950.

L'auteur, critique, acteur, metteur en scène, peintre et poète français, Jean Cocteau, sur un cheval de manège, 1950.

Robert Ranke
Graves at a café in
Palma, Majorca,
1954. He had
settled on the island
eight years earlier –
and lived to see its
peace wrecked
by tourists.

Robert Ranke
Graves in einem
Café in Palma de
Mallorca, 1954. Seit
acht Jahren lebte er
auf der Insel und
mußte miterleben,
wie sie mit Ankunft
der Touristen ihre
Beschaulichkeit
verlor.

Robert Ranke
Graves dans un café
de Palma, Majorque,
1954. Installé sur
l'île depuis huit ans,
il vit l'endroit perdre
peu à peu de sa
tranquillité avec
l'arrivée des
touristes.

Lucian Freud (left) and Brendan Behan chat together in a Dublin street, August 1952. It is possible that they shared a drink on that occasion.

Lucian Freud (links) und Brendan Behan im Gespräch in Dublin, August 1952. Vielleicht tranken sie bei dieser Gelegenheit noch etwas zusammen.

Lucian Freud (à gauche) et Brendan Behan en conversation dans une rue de Dublin, août 1952. Il est probable qu'ils profitèrent de l'occasion pour aller boire un verre.

Françoise Sagan on
a visit to London,
January 1958. She
was then 23 years
old and had already
published four
novels.

Françoise Sagan bei
einem Besuch in
London, 1958. Sie
war damals 23 Jahre
alt und hatte bereits
vier Romane ver-
öffentlicht.

Françoise Sagan en
visite à Londres,
janvier 1958. A 23
ans, elle avait déjà
publié quatre
romans.

Georges Enesco (foreground, right), composer, conductor, violinist and pianist, at the Bryanston Music School, August 1953.

Der Komponist, Dirigent, Violinist und Pianist Georges Enesco (rechts im Vordergrund) in der Bryanston Music School, August 1953.

Georges Enesco (au premier plan, à droite), compositeur, chef d'orchestre, violoniste et pianiste, à l'école de musique de Bryanston, août 1953.

Igor Stravinsky conducting, November 1959. By the Fifties, Stravinsky had turned to serial composition, with works such as *Canticum Sacrum*, *Agon* and *Threni*.

Igor Strawinsky dirigiert, November 1959. In den fünfziger Jahren hatte er sich mit Werken wie *Canticum Sacrum*, *Agon* und *Threni* der Zwölftonmusik zugewandt.

Igor Stravinski en répétition, novembre 1959. Dans les années cinquante, Stravinski se tourna vers la musique sérielle et composa des chefs-d'œuvre tels que *Canticum Sacrum*, *Agon* et *Threni*.

Venice, September 1954. (From left to right, backs against the wall) John Piper, Benjamin Britten and Peter Pears. They were relaxing from rehearsals of Britten's opera *The Turn of the Screw*, for which Piper was the set designer. The opera had its première in Venice.

Venedig, September 1954. (Von links nach rechts, an die Mauer gelehnt) John Piper, Benjamin Britten und Peter Pears in einer Probenpause während der Vorbereitung von Brittens Oper *The Turn of the Screw*. Piper entwarf für diese Inszenierung das Bühnenbild. Die Premiere fand in Venedig statt.

Venise, septembre 1954. (De gauche à droite, dos contre le mur) John Piper, Benjamin Britten et Peter Pears. Pause déjeuner pendant les répétitions de l'opéra de Britten *The Turn of the Screw*, dont Piper fut le décorateur. La première eut lieu à Venise.

Ralph Vaughan
Williams (left) and
Michael Tippett,
February 1958.
Vaughan Williams
died later that year,
Tippett in 1998.

Ralph Vaughan
Williams (links) und
Michael Tippett,
Februar 1958.
Vaughan Williams
verstarb noch im
selben Jahr,
Tippett 1998.

Ralph Vaughan
Williams (à gauche)
et Michael Tippett,
février 1958.
Vaughan Williams
mourut un an plus
tard, Tippett
en 1998.

The American Frank Lloyd Wright, probably the only architect to have a song written about him.

Der Amerikaner Frank Lloyd Wright war wohl der einzige Architekt, über den je ein Lied geschrieben wurde.

L'Américain Frank Lloyd Wright, probablement le seul architecte à être le sujet d'une chanson.

Wright's Guggenheim Museum in New York, 1955. The Guggenheim was one example of his 'organic architecture', based on the idea that buildings should seem to develop and grow from their surroundings. Critics called it arrogant, but Wright said he preferred 'honest arrogance' to 'hypocritical humility'.

Wrights Guggenheim Museum in New York, 1955. Das Guggenheim war ein Beispiel für „organische Architektur", basierend auf der Idee ein Gebäude sollte sich aus seiner Umgebung heraus entwickeln und formen. Kritiker bezeichneten diese Theorie als arrogant, doch Wright entgegnete nur, daß ihm „ehrliche Arroganz" lieber sei als „heuchlerische Bescheidenheit".

Le musée Guggenheim de Wright, New York, 1955. Guggenheim illustre l'« architecture organique » développée sur le principe qu'un bâtiment doit s'élever et prendre forme grâce à son environnement. Les critiques trouvaient cela arrogant mais Wright répondit qu'il préférait l'« arrogance honnête » à l'« humilité hypocrite ».

The Swiss-born French architect Le Corbusier in 1951, shortly after he had completed his Unité d'Habitation apartment-house project in Marseille, France.

Der in der Schweiz geborene französische Architekt Le Corbusier, 1951. Er hatte gerade sein Wohnhaus-Projekt Unité d'Habitation in Marseille fertiggestellt.

L'architecte français d'origine suisse Le Corbusier en 1951, peu de temps après avoir terminé son projet d'habitation à Marseille, les Unités d'Habitation.

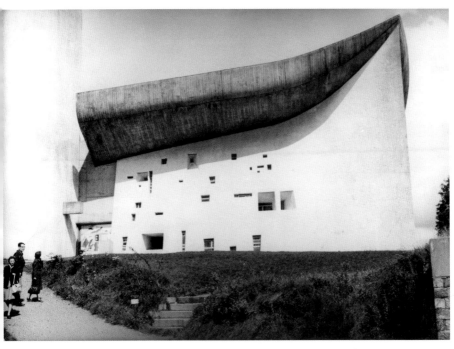

Le Corbusier's Chapel of Notre Dame de Haut, Ronchamp, 1955.
This was one of two religious buildings commissioned in the Fifties.
The most daring part of the concept was the roof, which appears to be
floating, but rests on a forest of supports.

Le Corbusiers Kapelle Notre Dame de Haut in Ronchamp, 1955. Sie
war eine der beiden Kirchen, die er in den fünfziger Jahren entwarf.
Der gewagteste Teil der Konstruktion war das Dach, das zu schweben
scheint und doch auf unzähligen Trägern ruht.

La chapelle Notre-Dame de Ronchamp du Corbusier, 1955.
Elle était l'une des deux églises commandées dans les années
cinquante. La partie la plus surprenante était le toit : il semble flotter
mais repose en fait sur de nombreux supports.

October 1950.
The Russian-born
architect and
designer Sir Misha
Black. This was the
year of his Dome of
Discovery for the
Festival of Britain.

Oktober 1950.
Der aus Rußland
stammende Archi-
tekt und Designer
Sir Misha Black. In
jenem Jahr ver-
wirklichte er seinen
Entwurf des Doms
der Entdeckungen
für das Festival of
Britain.

Octobre 1950.
L'architecte et
designer d'origine
russe Sir Misha
Black. Cette année-
là, il acheva le Dôme
de la découverte
pour le Festival
of Britain.

7 May 1951. Crowds queue on the south bank of the Thames for the opening ceremony of the Festival of Britain. The large building on the right was the Dome of Discovery, a predecessor of London's Millennium Dome. All that now remains of the Festival is the Concert Hall.

7. Mai 1951. Lange Menschenschlangen warten am südlichen Themse-Ufer auf den Einlaß zur Eröffnungszeremonie des Festival of Britain. Das große Gebäude zur Rechten war der Dom der Entdeckungen, ein Vorgänger des Londoner Millennium Dome. Das einzige heute noch erhaltene Gebäude ist die Konzerthalle.

7 mai 1951. Immenses files d'attente avant la cérémonie d'ouverture du Festival of Britain sur la rive Sud de la Tamise. Le grand bâtiment sur la droite est le Dôme de la découverte, le prédécesseur du Millennium Dome de Londres. Aujourd'hui, il ne reste plus qu'une salle de concert.

9. Fashion
Mode
La mode

August 1950. A model wearing a stylish dress of rayon-satin poses as though about to board a train. The photograph, which originally appeared in *Picture Post*, has the cautionary comment: 'An outfit like this is not for travelling, but for dressy occasions'.

August 1950. Ein Mannequin in einem eleganten Kleid aus Viskose-Satin posiert, als würde sie in einen Zug einsteigen wollen. Als die Aufnahme erstmals in der Zeitschrift *Picture Post* veröffentlicht wurde, war sie mit einem warnenden Hinweis versehen: „Diese Kleidung eignet sich nicht für eine Reise; sie ist für besondere Anlässe gedacht".

Août 1950. Un mannequin vêtue d'une élégante robe en satin et soie artificielle fait mine de monter dans le train. Cette photographie, publiée pour la première fois dans le *Picture Post* avait pour légende cette mise en garde : « Une tenue comme celle-ci n'est pas faite pour voyager mais pour les occasions habillées ».

9. Fashion
Mode
La mode

The presence of the United States was never removed from Europe after World War II. Paris and Milan reasserted their pre-eminence in the world of haute couture, but by the Fifties an alternative fashion, a fringe fashion, had appeared. All over the world it was 'hip', 'smart', and 'groovy' to wear the trappings of America. The young wanted crewcuts and sneakers, sweaters and slacks. They wanted to burn rubber in Thunderbirds and Chevvies, to drink shakes, to smoke Camels.

Meanwhile, the houses of Dior and Lanvin, Fabiani and Simonetta continued to set the length of hem and lapel, the depth of neckline, the width of sleeve. There was a return to the luxury of pre-war style, a recidivist elegance flaunted by glamorous models, and a hint of the Charleston age in the sack dress. Christian Dior died in 1957, and his modish shoes were filled by a precociously talented young student named Yves St Laurent.

Men in dark suits still paraded with rolled umbrellas and obligatory hats. At the end of a working day they changed into dinner jackets to visit the opera or the theatre. After all, there was no need to let standards drop simply because one lived in the shadow of the bomb.

But, over the horizon, lay the Sixties.

Auch nach dem Ende des Zweiten Weltkrieges blieb der Einfluß der Vereinigten Staaten in Europa allgegenwärtig. Paris und Mailand behaupteten zwar erneut ihre zentrale Stellung in der Welt der Haute Couture, doch hatte sich in den fünfziger Jahren auch eine alternative Modeszene gebildet. Auf der ganzen Welt war es nun „hip", „Spitze" und „stark", sich mit amerikanischen Produkten zu umgeben. Die Jugendlichen riefen nach Bürstenschnitten und Freizeitschuhen, amerikanischen Pullovern und Hosen. Sie träumten von Thunderbirds und Chevrolets, von Milch-Shakes und Camel-Zigaretten.

Unterdessen bestimmten die großen Modehäuser Dior und Lanvin, Fabiani und Simonetta nach wie vor die Länge des Saumes, die Breite des Aufschlags, die Tiefe des Ausschnitts und die Weite der Ärmel. Der verschwenderische Stil der Vorkriegszeit kehrte zurück, glamouröse Mannequins setzten die frühere Eleganz in Szene, und mit dem Sackkleid kam wieder ein Hauch der Charleston-Ära auf. Als Christian Dior 1957 starb, nahm ein vielversprechender junger Modeschüler namens Yves St. Laurent seinen Platz ein.

Herren in dunklen Anzügen spazierten noch immer mit Regenschirmen und obligatorischen Hüten durch die Straßen und schlüpften am Abend in Smokingjacken für einen Theater- oder Opernbesuch. Schließlich bestand kein Anlaß, seine Wertvorstellungen aufzugeben, nur weil inzwischen der Schatten der Wasserstoffbombe auf den Menschen lag.

Doch jenseits des Horizonts warteten bereits die sechziger Jahre.

Après la Seconde Guerre mondiale, l'influence des Etats-Unis persista en Europe. Certes, Paris et Milan réaffirmaient leur prééminence dans le monde de la haute couture mais, avec les années cinquante, une mode alternative et marginale vit le jour. Le style vestimentaire américain faisait fureur dans le monde entier, c'était « sensass » et « dans le vent ». Les jeunes se faisaient couper les cheveux en brosse et portaient des tennis, des pulls et des pantalons. Ils voulaient faire crisser les pneus d'une Thunderbird ou d'une Chevrolet, boire des milk-shakes et fumer des Camel.

Pendant ce temps, les maisons Dior, Lanvin, Fabiani et Simonetta continuaient d'imposer la longueur de l'ourlet, la profondeur du décolleté et la largeur de la manche. Il y avait un retour au luxe d'avant-guerre, une élégance recréée et portée par de superbes mannequins et, avec la robe sac, un clin d'œil à l'époque du charleston. Christian Dior mourut en 1957; un jeune étudiant au talent précoce, Yves Saint Laurent, prit le relais.

Quant aux messieurs en costumes sombres, ils continuaient d'aller et venir, parapluie sous le bras et, bien sûr, l'inévitable chapeau sur la tête. Leur journée de travail terminée, ils enfilaient un smoking pour se rendre à l'opéra ou au théâtre. Après tout, il n'y avait aucune raison d'abandonner les valeurs de référence sous prétexte qu'on vivait sous la menace de la bombe atomique.

Mais, à l'horizon, se profilaient les années soixante.

Two models (above) pose languorously in a cutaway Simca Aronde at the Paris Motor Show, October 1956. The British fashion model Ann Gunning (right) poses for a magazine cover in a 1952 knitted dress.

Zwei Mannequins (oben) posieren verführerisch in einem Simca Aronde ohne Türen auf der Automobilausstellung von Paris, Oktober 1956. Das britische Model Ann Gunning (rechts) posiert 1952 in einem Strickkleid für die Titelseite einer Zeitschrift.

Deux mannequins (ci-dessus) posent langoureusement dans une Simca Aronde aux portes découpées, Salon de l'Automobile, Paris, octobre 1956. Le mannequin britannique, Ann Gunning (à droite) pose pour la couverture d'un magazine vêtue d'une robe en tricot, 1952.

A classic early Fifties suit by Christian Dior, accentuating the waist. The ideal shape for a fashionable woman was to be tall and slim – some things never change.

Ein klassisches Kostüm der frühen fünfziger Jahre von Christian Dior. Die Taille wurde stark betont, und die modebewußte Dame sollte groß und schlank sein – manche Dinge ändern sich nie.

Taille mise en valeur avec cet ensemble de Christian Dior, typique du début des années cinquante. La taille idéale pour une femme qui se voulait à la mode était d'être grande et mince – preuve que certaines choses ne changeront jamais.

Second-hand glamour. A chic Parisienne sips her apéritif in a street café, but she is wearing a mass-produced version of a fashionable British dress.

Second-hand-Glamour. Eine modebewußte Pariserin, die in einem Straßencafé an einem Aperitif nippt, trägt ein nach einem britischen Modell kopiertes Kleid von der Stange.

Elégance de deuxième main. Cette Parisienne chic, assise à la terrasse d'un café et buvant un apéritif, porte une robe produite industriellement et copiée d'après un modèle britannique.

The prototype, April 1955. The design is by Jacques Fath, the setting is Paris, but the ensemble will soon be copied by others and produced by the thousand.

Der Prototyp, April 1955. Jacques Fath entwarf dieses Kleid, der Schauplatz ist Paris. Dieses Arrangement sollte bald kopiert und tausendfach nachproduziert werden.

Le prototype, avril 1955. Le styliste est Jacques Fath, le décor Paris mais l'ensemble sera très vite copié par d'autres et reproduit des milliers de fois.

February 1953.
A Parisian audience
of international
buyers critically
scans the work of a
British designer,
John Kavanagh.

Februar 1953.
Eine internationale
Klientel in Paris
begutachtet kritisch
die Arbeiten des
britischen Mode-
designers John
Kavanagh.

Février 1953.
Un parterre de
clientes du monde
entier à Paris
détaillant avec soin
le travail du styliste
britannique John
Kavanagh.

April 1955. High fashion in a rich setting. The gown is by Balenciaga, the background is Sa Majesté Salon de Thé, Paris.

April 1955. Hochmodische Kleidung in einer eleganten Umgebung. Das Abendkleid ist von Balenciaga, den passenden Hintergrund gibt der Pariser Teesalon Sa Majesté ab.

Avril 1955. Haute couture dans un quartier chic. La robe est de Balenciaga et le décor Sa Majesté, un salon de thé à Paris.

August 1954.
Maxime de la
Falaise models her
own designs for the
English market
– a pale tangerine
sweater and tie, with
apricot doeskin
pants.

August 1954.
Maxime de la
Falaise führt dem
englischen Mode-
markt ihre eigenen
Entwürfe vor – ein
orangefarbener
Pullover und
Krawatte mit einer
apricotfarbenen
Hose aus Rehleder.

Août 1954. Maxime
de la Falaise porte sa
propre collection
destinée au marché
anglais – un pull
avec nœud de
couleur mandarine
clair et des pantalons
en peau de daim
couleur abricot.

The French couturier Christian Dior at work in his Paris studio, June 1952. Almost single-handedly he reshaped post-war fashion.

Der französische Couturier Christian Dior bei der Arbeit in seinem Pariser Studio, Juni 1952. Er kreierte nahezu alleine die gesamte Nachkriegsmode.

Le couturier français Christian Dior dans son atelier à Paris, juin 1952. C'est lui seul ou presque qui créa la mode de l'après-guerre.

Dior's successor,
Yves St Laurent,
with the Dior top
model, Kouka,
after presenting his
winter collection in
Paris, 1959.

Diors Nachfolger
Yves St. Laurent mit
dem Topmodel des
Hauses Dior, Kouka,
nach der Vorstellung
seiner Winter-Kol-
lektion in Paris,
1959.

Le successeur de
Dior, Yves Saint
Laurent, en com-
pagnie du manne-
quin vedette de
Dior, Kouka, après
la présentation de sa
collection d'hiver,
Paris, 1959.

10. Youth
Die Jugend
La jeunesse

May 1954. The terrors and tearaways of the age. A 'Teddy boy' lights up at the Mecca Dance Hall, Tottenham, London. Teddy boys were so called because they adopted a neo-Edwardian style of dress, with drainpipe trousers and frock coats.

Mai 1954. Der Schrecken der Gesellschaft der fünfziger Jahre. Ein „Teddy-Boy" zündet sich eine Zigarette an vor der Mecca Dance Hall, Tottenham, London. Ihren Spitznamen verdankten die „Teddy-Boys" ihrer Kleidung, die mit Röhrenhosen und Gehröcken an die Zeit Eduards VII. erinnerte.

Mai 1954. Les terreurs et les casse-cou de l'époque. Un « Teddy-boy » s'allume une cigarette devant le Mecca, un dancing à Tottenham, Londres. On les appelait « teddy-boys » à cause de leur style post-Belle Epoque, de leurs pantalons-cigarette et de leurs redingotes.

10. Youth
Die Jugend
La jeunesse

As they passed from childhood to adulthood, adolescents in the Fifties suddenly found themselves labelled 'youths'. It was a totally new concept, a period of transition sandwiched between dependency and responsibility. For the first time in history teenagers had their own role models and music, fashion and language. If you weren't 'with it, Daddy-o', you were a 'square'. They even had their own meeting places – coffee bars in Europe, soda fountains in the United States.

At the heart of the new culture was a new music – Rock 'n' Roll. In retrospect there seems little in the hits of Bill Haley, Duane Eddy, Gene Vincent and Little Richard to threaten the established order. But politicians, ministers of religion and even psychiatrists roundly condemned the new sound as anarchic, demonic, or lunatic. There was dancing in the aisles and fainting in the stalls at Rock 'n' Roll concerts, and a whole lotta screaming going on, but it hardly matched the Bolshevik Revolution.

What was different was that the product – be it music or make-up, frothy coffee or bootlace neckwear – was aimed solely at young people. It didn't belong to children or to adults. For the first time young people tasted power in the market place, and they liked it.

Heranwachsende, die sich im Übergang von Kindheit zum Erwachsenenalter befanden, wurden in den fünfziger Jahren unvermittelt mit einer neuen Identität konfrontiert. Man nannte sie „Jugendliche". Daß zwischen der Zeit der Abhängigkeit und der Zeit der Eigenverantwortung eine Übergangsperiode lag, war eine völlig neue Vorstellung. Zum ersten Mal in der Geschichte der Menschheit hatten Teenager ihre eigenen Vorbilder, ihre eigene Musik, Mode und Sprache. Wer das nicht verstand, war „von gestern". Die Jugendlichen hatten sogar ihre eigenen Treffpunkte – Cafés in Europa, Erfrischungshallen in Amerika .

Das Kernstück dieser neuen Kultur bildete eine neue Musik – der Rock 'n' Roll. Aus heutiger Sicht kann man in den Hits von Bill Haley, Duane Eddy, Gene Vincent und Little Richard kaum eine Bedrohung erkennen, doch damals verurteilten Politiker, Geistliche und selbst Psychiater den neuen Klang als anarchistisch, dämonisch und verrückt. Bei Rock-'n'-Roll-Konzerten wurde zwar in den Gängen getanzt und nach Leibeskräften geschrien, viele junge Frauen fielen sogar in Ohnmacht, doch ein Vergleich mit der bolschewistischen Revolution lag nicht unbedingt nahe.

Das einzig Neue jener Zeit war, daß sich das Produkt – ob Make-up, Musik, Cappuccino oder Schnürsenkel-Schmuck – ausschließlich an die Zielgruppe junger Leute richtete. Diese Dinge betrafen weder Kinder noch Erwachsene. Zum ersten Mal spürte die Jugend ihre Macht auf dem Weltmarkt, und sie genoß dieses Gefühl.

Dans les années cinquante, les adolescents qui sortaient de l'enfance pour entrer dans l'âge adulte se retrouvèrent soudain classés dans la catégorie « jeunes ». C'était un concept totalement nouveau, faisant référence à la période de transition entre la dépendance et la responsabilité. Pour la première fois, les adolescents adoptaient des modèles, une musique, une mode et un langage qui leur étaient propres. Si vous n'étiez pas « dans le coup », vous étiez « vieux jeu ». Les jeunes avaient aussi leurs propres lieux de rencontre – cafés en Europe, bars à soda aux Etats-Unis.

Au cœur de cette nouvelle culture, une musique nouvelle faisait rage – le rock'n'roll. Il suffit de ré-écouter les tubes de Bill Haley, Duane Eddy, Gene Vincent et Little Richard pour comprendre qu'ils ne menaçaient pas l'ordre établi. Mais, à l'époque, des politiciens, des hommes d'Eglise et même des psychiatres condamnèrent à tour de rôle ce genre de musique, jugé anarchiste, démoniaque ou aliénant. Dans les salles de concert de rock, on avait beau danser, s'évanouir et hurler beaucoup, il n'y avait pas de quoi invoquer une révolution bolchévique.

La nouveauté était que le produit – tant la musique, le maquillage que le cappuccino ou un collier en lacets de chaussure – s'adressait uniquement aux adolescents. Il n'était destiné ni aux enfants ni aux adultes. Pour la première fois, les jeunes prirent conscience qu'ils pouvaient influencer le marché et cela leur plut.

Not just a pale imitation of the transatlantic 'real thing' – an early picture of British rock-and-roll singer Tommy Steele, who made his professional debut in October 1956.

Nicht nur eine schlechte Imitation des wahren King of Rock 'n' Roll jenseits des Atlantiks – eine frühe Aufnahme des britischen Sängers Tommy Steele, der im Oktober 1956 seinen ersten Bühnenauftritt hatte.

Plus qu'une pâle imitation de ce qui se faisait outre-Atlantique – il s'agit du chanteur de rock britannique Tommy Steele lors de ses débuts sur scène, octobre 1956.

February 1959.
19-year-old Cliff
Richard sends his
fans wild with
delight, Cliff had
had his first big hit –
Schoolboy Crush –
just five months
earlier.

Februar 1959. Schon
mit 19 Jahren
brachte Cliff
Richard seine Fans
aus der Fassung.
Fünf Monate zuvor
hatte der Sänger
einen ersten großen
Hit mit *Schoolboy
Crush*.

février 1959. Cliff
Richard, âgé de 19
ans, fait le bonheur
de ses fans. Son
premier grand tube
– *Schoolboy Crush* –
était sorti cinq mois
plus tôt.

Fans of Johnnie 'Cry Guy' Ray show the agony and ecstasy of their adoration. Ray thanked his fans for their understanding – they never touched his hearing aid.

Verehrerinnen des Sängers Johnnie „Cry Guy" Ray lassen ihren Gefühlen freien Lauf. Ray dankte seinen Fans für ihr Verständnis – sie hielten stets Abstand von seinem Hörgerät.

Des fans de Johnnie « Cry Guy » Ray affichent le désespoir et l'extase de leur adoration. Ray remercia ses fans pour leur compréhension – personne ne toucha à son appareil auditif.

February 1957. Bill Haley (second from right) and his Comets on stage at the Dominion Theatre, London. 'Every member of the Comets represents a denial of the so-called "delinquency" label attached by some killjoys to rock-and-roll…' – *New Musical Express*.

Februar 1957. Bill Haley (zweiter von rechts) und seine Comets auf der Bühne des Dominion Theatre in London. „Jedes Bandmitglied der Comets ist ein Beweis dafür, daß das Etikett der „Delinquenz", das manche dem Rock 'n' Roll anhängen wollen, schlichtweg nicht zutrifft …" – *New Musical Express*.

Février 1957. Bill Haley (deuxième à droite) et ses Comets sur scène au Dominion Theatre de Londres. « Chaque joueur des Comets contredit l'image de pseudo-« délinquance » que certains rabat-joie veulent coller au rock'n'roll » – *New Musical Express*.

June 1959. Elvis Presley at a press conference in Paris. He was then on leave from the American army in Germany, stationed in Frankfurt, and had been promoted to Private First Class. His pay was $20 a month.

Juni 1959. Elvis Presley während einer Pressekonferenz in Paris. Er war gerade auf Urlaub vom Militärdienst bei der amerikanischen Armee in Deutschland, stationiert in Frankfurt, und war zum Obergefreiten befördert worden. Sein Gehalt betrug 20 $ pro Monat.

Juin 1959. Elvis Presley lors d'une conférence de presse à Paris. Basé à Francfort, il avait obtenu une permission de l'armée américaine qui venait de le nommer « soldat de première classe » avec un salaire de 20 $ par mois.

Fifteen-year-old John Lennon with The Quarrymen at their first gig, at
Woolton, near Liverpool, June 1955. The band members are (from left to right)
Eric Griffiths, Rod Davies, John Lennon, Pete Shotton and Len Garry.

John Lennon im Alter von 15 Jahren mit The Quarrymen bei ihrem ersten
Auftritt in Woolton, in der Nähe von Liverpool, Juni 1955. Die Bandmitglieder
waren (von links nach rechts) Eric Griffiths, Rod Davies, John Lennon, Pete
Shotton und Len Garry.

John Lennon, âgé de 15 ans, avec les Quarrymen lors de leur premier concert, à
Woolton, près de Liverpool, juin 1955. Les membres du groupe sont (de gauche
à droite) Eric Griffiths, Rod Davies, John Lennon, Pete Shotton et Len Garry.

October 1954. Gas-guzzlers of the Fifties. The proud owner of a chrome-encrusted Buick seeks to impress a young woman.

Oktober 1954. Ein Benzinschlucker der fünfziger Jahre. Der stolze Eigentümer dieses chrom-verzierten Buicks versucht offenbar, eine junge Frau zu beeindrucken.

Octobre 1954. La grosse consomma-trice d'essence dans les années cinquante. Le propriétaire de cette Buick chromée, fier comme un paon, cherche à épater cette jeune femme.

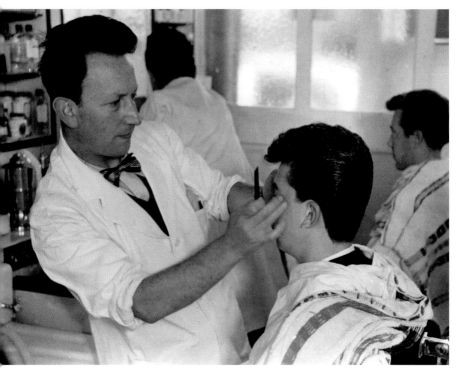

November 1954. A cut above the rest. Hairdresser Mr Rose, who claimed to have been the inventor of the 'quiff', goes to work on a young customer. Gone were the days of 'short back and sides'.

November 1954. Diese Frisur ist allen anderen überlegen. Mr. Rose, der für sich in Anspruch nahm, der Erfinder der „Tolle" zu sein, stylt einen jungen Kunden. Vorbei die Zeiten, in denen man sein Haar „hinten und an den Seiten kurz" trug.

Novembre 1954. Plus court que tout. Le coiffeur, M. Rose, qui déclare avoir inventé la « banane » se met à l'œuvre sur un jeune client. Finie l'époque de la coupe « court derrière et sur les côtés ».

Classic clothes, classic pose. A young Teddy boy displays his 'gear' in Tottenham, London, May 1954.

Klassische Kleidung, klassische Pose. Ein junger Teddy-Boy präsentiert seinen Schick in Tottenham, London, Mai 1954.

Tenue classique, pose classique. Un jeune Teddy-boy affiche son style à Tottenham, Londres, mai 1954.

November 1950.
A young aspirant
checks his
appearance at the
Rank School for
Cinema Managers,
Finchley, London.
The mirror has
arrows indicating
dress code.

November 1950.
Ein hoffnungsvoller
Kandidat überprüft
seine Erscheinung in
der Rank-Schule für
Kino-Manager,
Finchley, London.
Auf dem Spiegel
befinden sich Be-
kleidungsregeln.

Novembre 1950.
Un jeune candidat
vérifie sa tenue à
l'Ecole des
directeurs de cinéma
de Rank, Finchley,
Londres. Des flèches
sur le miroir
indiquent des codes
vestimentaires.

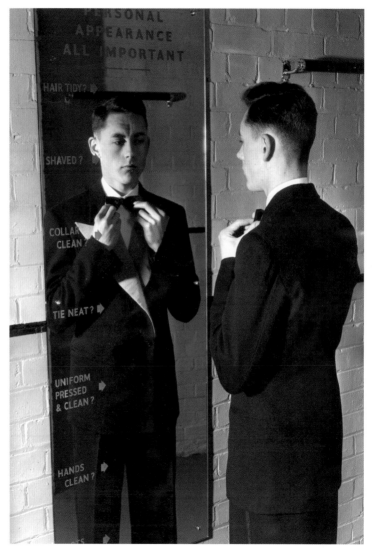

May 1954. 'Teds' get together on a night out at the Mecca Dance Hall,
Tottenham, London. Like rock-and-rollers, Teddy boys were seen by
many as delinquents, but their main preoccupations (dancing, dressing
up and drinking) were harmless enough.

Mai 1954. „Teds" feiern einen Abend in der Mecca Dance Hall,
Tottenham, London. Viele sahen wie in den Rock-'n'-Rollern auch in
den Teddy-Boys potentielle Delinquenten, obwohl ihre Haupt-
interessen (tanzen, schicke Kleidung und trinken) eher harmlos waren.

Mai 1954. Soirée pour « teds » au Mecca, un nightclub de Tottenham,
Londres. Les teddy-boys, tout comme les rockers, étaient considérés
par beaucoup comme des délinquants mais leurs préoccupations
essentielles (danser, s'habiller et boire) étaient plutôt innocentes.

Innocents in Soho, 1957.
Four young women, who styled themselves 'The Kittens', perform their version of the 'hand jive' in a coffee bar to music from The Bell Cats.

Unschuldslämmer in Soho, 1957. Vier junge Frauen, die sich „Die Kätzchen" nennen, führen in einem Café zur Musik der Bell Cats ihre Version des „Hand-Swings" vor.

Innocentes à Soho, 1957. Quatre jeunes filles, dites les « Chatons », exécutent leur propre « jeu de mains » dans un café, accompagnées du groupe The Bell Cats.

Members of the
British branch of the
Liberace Fan Club
relax, August 1956.
Liberace first hit the
charts a year earlier
with his piano
version of
Unchained Melody.

Anhänger des
britischen Liberace-
Fanclubs entspannen
sich, August 1956.
Liberace stürmte ein
Jahr zuvor zum
ersten Mal die
Hitparaden mit
seiner Klavierversion
des Liedes
Unchained Melody.

Détente pour des
membres du fan club
britannique de
Liberace, août 1956.
Liberace avait atteint
le sommet des hit-
parades un an plus
tôt avec sa version
piano de *Unchained
Melody*.

By 1955, when this picture was taken, juke boxes were installed in many pubs and coffee bars throughout Europe as well as all over the United States. They were not seen as supplying background noise – teenagers really listened to the music they provided.

Als diese Aufnahme 1955 entstand, gab es bereits Musikautomaten in zahlreichen Lokalen und Cafés überall in Europa und den Vereinigten Staaten. Damals diente Musik nicht nur zur Unterhaltung – die Teenager hörten sie sich aufmerksam an.

En 1955, date à laquelle ce cliché fut pris, les juke boxes avaient déjà fait leur apparition dans de nombreux pubs et cafés d'Europe et des Etats-Unis. Ils ne servaient pas uniquement de musique d'ambiance – les adolescents écoutaient avec attention la musique sélectionnée.

Saturday Night Fever, October 1952. Somewhere – a thousand kisses away – the lights are sparkling, the band is playing, and couples are dancing on the floor of the Astoria Ballroom, Nottingham. But in the shadows, passion erupts.

Saturday Night Fever, Oktober 1952. Irgendwo – tausend Küsse entfernt – flackern die Lichter, spielt die Band und tanzen Paare im Astoria-Tanzsaal, Nottingham. In den dunklen Ecken entflammt jedoch die Leidenschaft.

La fièvre du samedi soir, octobre 1952. Quelque part – à des milliers de baisers – les lumières brillent, l'orchestre joue et des couples dansent sur la piste de l'Astoria, un dancing de Nottingham. Mais, dans l'ombre, la passion éclate.

Fugitives from the party, 1955. The venue is
an artist's house in Chelsea, London. In the
backyard, two minds and two hearts have but
a single thought.

Von der Party geflüchtet, 1955. Im Haus eines
Künstlers in Chelsea, London, findet zwar ein
Fest statt, doch diese beiden Verliebten
im Hinterhof haben nur einen Gedanken.

Fugitifs loin de la fête organisée dans la
maison d'un artiste de Chelsea, Londres,
1955. Dans la cour, deux êtres et deux cœurs
n'ont qu'une pensée en tête.

11. Science
Wissenschaft
La science

'To boldly go where no ex-king has gone before…' Peter of Yugoslavia, dethroned in 1945, prepares to enter the 'Space machine' with his son, Prince Alexander, at the Schoolboys' Own Exhibition, Horticultural Hall, Westminster, London, December 1953.

„Dorthin gehen, wo kein Ex-König je zuvor war…" Peter von Jugoslawien, entthront 1945, ist bereit, mit seinem Sohn, Prinz Alexander, die „Weltraummaschine" auf einer Schülerausstellung zu betreten, Horticultural Hall, Westminster, London, Dezember 1953.

« Aller là où aucun roi n'a jamais été … » Pierre de Yougoslavie, détrôné en 1945, prêt à monter dans la « Machine de l'espace » avec son fils, le prince Alexandre, lors d'une exposition pour enfants à Horticultural Hall, Westminster, Londres, décembre 1953.

11. Science
   Wissenschaft
   La science

The Space Age was just around the corner. The United States launched their *Pioneer* rocket in October 1958, but it failed to reach the moon. Three months later, the Soviet Union's *Lunik I* shot nearly 350,000 miles into space. But, for most of the Fifties, scientists and boffins had to be content with other new toys – flying bedsteads, 3D movies, and the largest radio telescope in the world at Jodrell Bank.

CBS began television transmissions in colour in 1951, but sets cost $1,300 – six months' wages for the average worker. The first non-iron polyester appeared in 1955. Smoking was linked to cancer. The first sex-change operation took place in 1952. Two years later the first human pregnancy was achieved using previously frozen sperm.

Drugs were regularly tested on animals. Nuclear fall-out was tested on human beings. In both cases the guinea pigs had not the slightest idea what was happening to them. Not surprisingly, many felt human intelligence needed artificial back-up, and rival companies raced to produce a working electronic brain. The prototypes were about the size of a ballroom.

Das Raumzeitalter stand unmittelbar bevor. Die Vereinigten Staaten starteten im Oktober 1958 ihre Rakete *Pioneer*, sie erreichte jedoch nicht den Mond. Drei Monate später schoß die sowjetische Mondsonde *Lunik I* fast 560.000 Kilometer tief in den Weltraum. Die meiste Zeit der fünfziger Jahre mußten sich Wissenschaftler und Tüftler jedoch mit anderen neuen Spielzeugen zufriedengeben – Fluggeräte, wie das Fliegende Bettgestell, 3D-Filme und das größte Radioteleskop der Welt in der Forschungsstation Jodrell Bank.

CBS begann im Jahre 1951 zwar mit Fernsehübertragungen in Farbe, aber die Geräte, die man für den Empfang benötigte, kosteten 1.300 $ – das entsprach etwa dem halben Jahreslohn. Der erste bügelfreie Polyesterstoff kam 1955 auf den Markt, und man erkannte den

Zusammenhang zwischen Krebserkrankungen und Tabakkonsum. 1952 wurde die erste operative Geschlechtsumwandlung vorgenommen, und zwei Jahre später wurde das erste menschliche Embryo mit Hilfe zuvor eingefrorenen Spermas gezeugt.

Medikamente und Kosmetika wurden in Tierversuchen getestet, radioaktiver Niederschlag am Menschen. In beiden Fällen hatten die Versuchskaninchen nicht die geringste Ahnung, was mit ihnen geschah. Es überrascht daher nicht, daß man vielerorts der Ansicht war, man benötigte zur Ergänzung der menschlichen Intelligenz eine künstliche. Rivalisierende Firmen lieferten sich nunmehr ein Rennen in der Entwicklung des ersten Elektronenhirns. Die Prototypen waren etwa so groß wie ein Tanzsaal.

L'âge de l'espace approchait. En octobre 1958, les Etats-Unis lançaient la fusée *Pioneer* mais elle n'atteignit pas la lune. Trois mois plus tard, le *Lunik I* des Soviétiques parcourait plus de 560 000 kilomètres dans l'espace. Mais les scientifiques et chercheurs des années cinquante durent se contenter d'autres nouveaux jouets – engins volants, films en trois dimensions et le plus grand radiotéléscope du monde à Jodrell Bank.

CBS commença à émettre en couleur dès 1951; à cette époque, un téléviseur couleur coûtait 1.300 $, l'équivalent de six mois de salaire d'un ouvrier. En 1955, le premier polyester sans repassage fit son apparition tandis qu'on établissait le lien entre cancer et cigarette. En 1952 eut lieu la première opération pour changer de sexe. Deux ans plus tard, la première grossesse réalisée avec des spermes préalablement congelés fut menée à terme.

Les médicaments étaient régulièrement testés sur les animaux. Les retombées radioactives étaient testées sur les hommes. Dans les deux cas, les cobayes n'avaient pas la moindre idée de ce qu'on leur faisait subir. Il n'est donc pas surprenant qu'un grand nombre de gens éprouvèrent soudain le besoin de créer un support artificiel pour l'intelligence humaine. Les entreprises rivales se lancèrent aussitôt dans la course pour fabriquer le premier cerveau électronique. Les prototypes avaient presque la taille d'une salle de bal.

Laika is strapped into *Sputnik II* before take-off for space, 5 November 1957. She had a one-way ticket, for the rocket was not designed to return to earth, and the dog died when her oxygen supply ran out.

Laika wird vor dem Start in den Weltraum in der *Sputnik II* ange-schnallt, 5. November 1957. Sie hatte nur ein Ticket für die Hinfahrt, denn diese Rakete war nicht dazu bestimmt, zur Erde zurückzukehren, und die Hündin starb, als die Sauerstoffreserve erschöpft war.

Laïka, attachée à l'intérieur de *Spoutnik II* avant son décollage dans l'espace, 5 novembre 1957. Elle n'avait qu'un aller simple car la fusée n'avait pas été conçue pour regagner la Terre. La chienne mourut une fois la réserve d'oxygène épuisée.

In December 1959, Sam was luckier. The rhesus monkey had only a 13-minute trip in space before being parachuted back to earth, where he landed safely and apparently suffered no ill effects.

Sam hatte im Dezember 1959 etwas mehr Glück. Die Reise des Rhesusaffen in den Weltraum währte nur 13 Minuten, bevor er mit einem Fallschirm sicher und scheinbar unversehrt wieder auf der Erde landete.

En décembre 1959, Sam fut plus chanceux. Le voyage du macaque dans l'espace ne dura que 13 minutes. Il put ensuite regagner la Terre en parachute où il atterrit sans encombre. Apparement, il ne ressentit aucun effet secondaire.

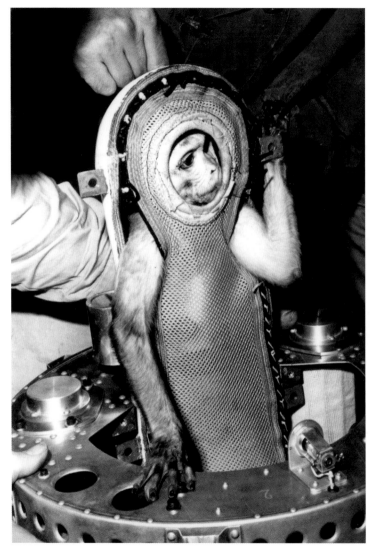

Gillingham, Kent, 1958. Years ahead of Tereshkova (the first woman in space) five-year-old Linda Chapman enters her toy rocket during New Year's Eve celebrations at the NAAFI Club.

Gillingham, Kent, 1958. Die fünf-jährige Linda Chapman war Tereschkowa (die erste Frau im Weltraum), um Jahre voraus, als sie auf der Silvester-party des Clubs der britischen Armee (NAAFI) in ihre Spielzeugrakete kletterte.

Gillingham, Kent, 1958. Bien des années avant Tereshkova (la première femme dans l'espace), Linda Chapman, cinq ans, monte dans sa fusée installée dans le club d'une coopérative militaire (NAAFI) lors d'une fête de fin d'année.

Wernher von Braun, 1958. From 1950 onwards, von Braun was the guiding light of the United States space programme. He had pioneered the liquid-fuelled rocket, and as early as 1952 predicted that it would be possible to explore Mars.

Wernher von Braun, 1958. Ab 1950 oblag von Braun die Leitung der amerikanischen Raumfahrtforschung. Er leistete Pionierarbeit auf dem Gebiet der Flüssigrakete und erkannte bereits 1952, daß es möglich sein werde, den Mars zu erforschen.

Wernher von Braun, 1958. Il fut dès 1950 le grand initiateur du programme spatial des Etats-Unis. Il avait conçu la première fusée à combustion liquide et affirma dès 1952 qu'il serait un jour possible d'explorer Mars.

New Mexico's primary industry. A US Air Force TM-76 missile screams out of its launch pad in the desert, August 1959. The Cold War was then at its most frigid.

Die Hauptindustrie New Mexicos. Eine TM-76-Rakete der amerikanischen Luftwaffe schießt von der Startrampe, August 1959. Der Kalte Krieg hatte seinen Höhepunkt erreicht.

Industrie principale du Nouveau Mexique. Un missile TM-76 de l'armée américaine lancé avec grand fracas hors de sa base de décollage dans le désert, août 1959. La guerre froide en était à son stade le plus glacé.

The Flying
Coléoptère
('beetle'), propelled
by a turbo-reactor to
take off and
land vertically,
Melun, near Paris,
July 1958.

Der fliegende
Coléoptère
(„Käfer") wurde von
einem Turboreaktor
angetrieben und
konnte senkrecht
starten und landen,
Melun, bei Paris, Juli
1958.

Le coléoptère volant
(« scarabée »),
propulsé par un
turbo-réacteur,
décolle et atterrit à
la verticale, Melun,
près de Paris, juillet
1958.

The Flying Bedstead, England, August 1954. Its proper name was the Rolls-Royce Thrust Measuring Rig, a title as ungainly as its looks. It was the first vertical take-off aircraft, but not a machine for flying in wet weather.

Das Fliegende Bettgestell, England, August 1954. Offiziell hieß es „Rolls-Royce Schubmeßanlage", ein Name, der so unschön war wie das Vehikel selbst. Es war das erste Luftfahrzeug, das senkrecht starten konnte, nur bei Regenwetter war es nicht zu empfehlen.

Engin volant, Angleterre, août 1954. Plus officiellement il fut appelé, « plate-forme de contrôle Rolls-Royce », titre aussi disgracieux que son apparence. Cet appareil, le premier à décoller verticalement, n'était pas recommandé par temps de pluie.

Alice in Horrorland. A line of white rabbits undergoing a Pyrogen test at a chemical research centre, 1956. The test was to determine the drug's suitablilty for humans. Few worried about its suitability for rabbits.

Alice im Horrorland. Weiße Kaninchen werden in einem chemischen Forschungszentrum einem Pyrogen-Test unterzogen, 1956. In diesem Test sollte die Verträglichkeit der Substanz für Menschen ermittelt werden. Ob die Kaninchen sie vertrugen, hat damals kaum jemanden interessiert.

Alice au pays des horreurs. Test de pyrogène sur des lapins blancs dans un laboratoire pharmaceutique, 1956. Ce test devait permettre de déterminer si ce médicament était adapté aux êtres humains. La question de savoir s'il était adapté aux animaux n'était pas vraiment à l'ordre du jour.

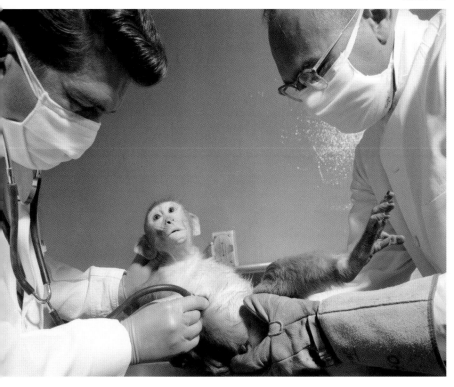

Meanwhile, further along the evolutionary chain, veterinarians
check the heartbeat of a monkey in a similar laboratory, also in 1956.
Animal welfare groups were few and far between in the Fifties.

Währenddessen, einige Stufen höher in der Evolution, prüfen zwei
Veterinärmediziner den Herzschlag eines kleinen Affen in einem
anderen Labor, 1956. Tierschützer waren in den fünfziger Jahren noch
eine Seltenheit.

Entre-temps, un peu plus loin sur la chaîne de l'évolution, dans un
autre centre de recherches, un vétérinaire écoute les battements de
cœur d'un petit singe, 1956. Les associations pour la défense des
animaux n'étaient pas nombreuses dans les années cinquante.

A tooth for a tooth… A patient examines a giant set of dentures used by a dental hygienist to demonstrate correct brushing methods, 1950.

Zahn um Zahn… Eine kleine Patientin untersucht ein riesiges Gebiß, anhand dessen der Zahnarzt ihr erklären wird, wie man die Zähne richtig putzt, 1950.

Dent pour dent … Une patiente examine un dentier géant, utilisé par un dentiste pour faire la démonstration de la bonne façon de se brosser les dents, 1950.

An eye for an eye...
A pupil at Oyster
Bay School, Long
Island, USA, uses a
'metronoscope'
to help his eyes
function, 1955.

Auge um Auge...
Ein amerikanischer
Schüler der Oyster
Bay School auf Long
Island, USA, benutzt
ein „Metronoskop",
um sein Sehver-
mögen zu ver-
bessern, 1955.

Œil pour œil ...
Un élève de l'école
d'Oyster Bay, Long
Island, Etats-Unis,
utilise un « métro-
oscope » pour
corriger sa vue,
1955.

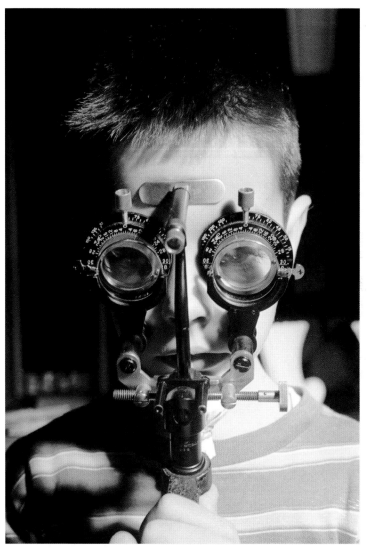

February 1955.
Testing the Ferranti
computer at
Moston,
Manchester. Nine
months earlier, IBM
had produced their
own electronic
brain.

Februar 1955.
Dieser Computer-
spezialist testet einen
Ferranti-Computer
in Moston, Man-
chester. Neun
Monate zuvor hatte
IBM bereits sein
eigenes Elektronen-
hirn entwickelt.

Février 1955.
Essai de l'ordinateur
Ferranti à Moston,
Manchester. Neuf
mois plus tôt, IBM
avait sorti son
premier cerveau
électronique.

Discovering how the brain works. In the Burden Neurological Institute, Bristol, a patient is connected to an encephalogram, March 1950. This was one of the first machines to record the brain's activity by reading its electric pulses.

Erforschen, wie das Gehirn arbeitet. Im Burden Neurological Institute in Bristol wird ein Enzephalogramm von einem Patienten erstellt, März 1950. Hier befand sich eines der ersten Geräte, das die Aktivität des Gehirns durch Aufzeichnung seiner elektrischen Impulse lesbar machen konnte.

Découvrir le fonctionnement du cerveau. En mars 1950, au Centre de neurologie de Burden à Bristol, un patient est branché sur un encéphalogramme, l'une des premières machines à pouvoir enregistrer l'activité du cerveau grâce à l'analyse de ses vibrations électriques.

April 1956.
Party political broadcast,
Italian style. A fleet of
cars, topped with giant
back-projection screens,
hits the road to take the
Christian Democratic
Union's message to the
electorate.

April 1956.
Parteipolitische Werbung
auf italienische Art.
Eine Wagenkolonne,
versehen mit riesigen
Bildschirmen, soll den
Wählern die Botschaft
der Christlich-Demo-
kratischen Union
vermitteln.

Avril 1956. Campagne
de l'Union chrétienne
démocrate, à l'italienne.
Une flotte de voitures,
surmontées d'écrans
géants, se met en route
pour diffuser le message
du parti à son électorat.

The lazy gardener's
delight. Pamela
Weller demonstrates
a radio-controlled
lawnmower, 1959.

Das Glück des
arbeitsscheuen
Gärtners. Pamela
Weller präsentiert
einen fernge-
steuerten Rasen-
mäher, 1959.

Le bonheur du
jardinier paresseux.
Pamela Weller fait la
démonstration d'une
tondeuse à gazon
télécommandée,
1959.

The world's smallest record player, 1958. The Fifties saw an enormous boom in the gramophone industry with the introduction of the 45rpm and 33rpm long-playing records. This machine may have been handy, but almost certainly lacked quality in the reproduction of sound.

Der kleinste Plattenspieler der Welt, 1958. In den fünfziger Jahren erlebte die Schallplattenindustrie einen ungeheuren Aufschwung durch die Einführung von Langspielplatten mit 45 oder 33 UpM. Dieses Gerät mag wohl praktisch gewesen sein, seine Klangwiedergabe ließ aber sicherlich einiges zu wünschen übrig.

Le plus petit tourne-disque du monde, 1958. Dans les années cinquante, l'industrie du disque connut un « boom » sans précédent avec l'arrivée des disques à 45 et à 33 tours. D'une taille certes pratique, la qualité du son de cet appareil laissait certainement à désirer.

A woman adjusts her smog mask before facing a London 'pea-souper',
1953. Another two years were to pass, however, before anti-smog
legislation gave inhabitants of cities anything like clean air.

Eine Frau mit Smogmaske macht sich zurecht, bevor sie sich in die
Londoner „Erbsensuppe" begibt, 1953. Es sollten noch zwei Jahre
vergehen, bis durch entsprechende Gesetze die Luft in den Städten
wieder erträglich wurde.

Cette femme ajuste son masque anti-brouillard avant de sortir dans la
« purée de pois » londonienne, 1953. Il fallut attendre encore deux ans
avant qu'une loi anti-smog ne permette d'améliorer un peu la qualité
de l'air dans les villes.

Visitors to the Festival of Britain on London's South Bank at a 3D cinema, 1951.
As television began to bite, the movie industry experimented with new techniques,
trying in turn 3D, Cinemascope ('You see it without glasses!'), and Cinerama.

Besucher des Londoner Festival of Britain in einem 3 D-Kino. Nachdem das
Fernsehen Fuß gefaßt hatte, experimentierte die Filmindustrie mit neuen
Techniken wie 3-D, Cinemascope („Diesen Effekt sehen Sie sogar ohne Brille!")
und Cinerama.

Spectateurs au Festival of Britain, Londres, au cinéma en 3 dimensions, 1951.
Alors que la télévision commençait à faire des adeptes, l'industrie du cinéma
expérimentait de nouvelles techniques, dont le cinéma en 3 dimensions, le
cinémascope (« que l'on peut voir sans lunettes! ») et le cinérama.

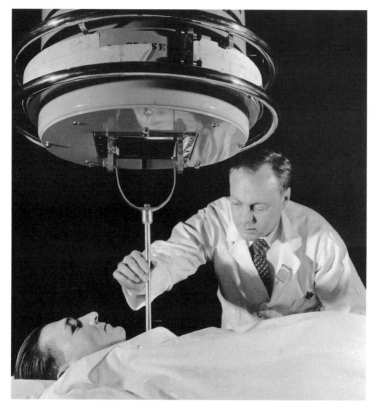

The Nuclear war against Cancer. A patient at the Delafield Hospital undergoes radiation treatment, 1955. Two million volts of deep therapy X-rays were radiated into the cancerous cells.

Der nukleare Kampf gegen Krebs. Ein Patient im Delafield Krankenhaus unterzieht sich einer radioaktiven Behandlung, 1955. Die krebshaften Zellen werden im Rahmen einer Röntgenstrahlen-Therapie mit zwei Millionen Volt bestrahlt.

La guerre nucléaire contre le cancer. Un patient à l'Hôpital Delafield subit un traitement de radiation, 1955. Les cellules cancéreuses étaient irradiées par deux millions de volts dans le cadre d'une thérapie à rayons X.

One of the millions
of schoolchildren
protected from polio
with the vaccine
developed by
Dr Jonas Salk of
Pittsburgh,
26 May 1956.

Eines von Millionen
von Schulkindern,
das mit dem von
Dr. Jonas Salk aus
Pittsburgh ent-
wickelten Impfstoff
vor Kinderlähmung
geschützt wird, 26.
Mai 1956.

L'un des millions
d'enfants à être
protégés contre la
polio par un vaccin
mis au point par le
Dr. Jonas Salk de
Pittsburgh, 26 mai
1956.

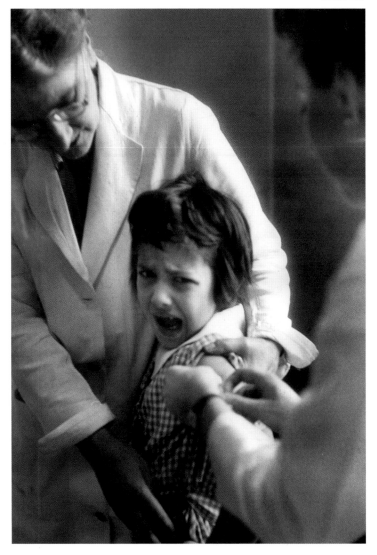

12. Transport
Transportwesen
Les moyens de transport

'Sin on two wheels' in John Sadovy's 1956 picture of scooter chic. It didn't give the most comfortable of rides, but for millions of young people the scooter offered independence and freedom at a bargain price, and, in this case, considerable allure.

„Sünde auf zwei Rädern" auf einer Aufnahme von John Sadovy, 1956. Eine Fahrt auf dem Motorroller war zwar nicht unbedingt bequem, doch für Millionen junger Leute bedeutete der Motorroller Unabhängigkeit und Freiheit zum Sonderpreis und, wie in diesem Fall, einen erheblichen Reiz.

« La tentation à deux roues » ou le chic en scooter, photographié par John Sadovy, 1956. Il y avait plus confortable pour se balader mais, pour des millions de jeunes, le scooter offrait indépendance et liberté à un prix exceptionnel et, comme ici, beaucoup d'allure.

12. Transport
Transportwesen
Les moyens de transport

It was one of transport's golden ages. Great liners still ploughed through the oceans of the world, giving seaborne luxury to the rich and idle. The SS *United States* was launched in May 1952, and within a couple of months had taken the Blue Riband for the fastest ever crossing of the Atlantic – in 3 days, 10 hours and 40 minutes.

The new Boeing 707 could do better than that. It was the first ever jumbo jet, and it could cruise with 189 passengers at 600 mph. The era of the package holiday had arrived. Airports bulged with first-time fliers. New York's La Guardia Airport announced with awe that it expected to handle 6.5 million passengers in a single year.

For the motorist there was a greater choice of vehicles than ever before, everything from the gull-winged Mercedes to the Heinkel bubble car. Detroit had a vast range of giant, gleaming saloons. Volkswagens beetled off the production lines in Germany. In Britain, Alec Issigonis designed the new Mini, and a motor-mad Conservative government provided motorists with Britain's first motorways.

Für das Transportwesen waren die fünfziger Jahre ein Goldenes Zeitalter. Ozeanriesen kreuzten noch immer über die Weltmeere und boten den wohlhabenden Müßiggängern verschwenderischen Luxus. Die SS *United States* lief im Mai 1952 vom Stapel und errang innerhalb von zwei Monaten das Blaue Band für die schnellste Atlantiküberquerung – sie benötigte 3 Tage, 10 Stunden und 40 Minuten.

Die neue Boeing 707 war da noch schneller. Sie war der erste Jumbojet und konnte 189 Fluggäste mit einer Reisegeschwindigkeit von 960 km/h befördern. Die ersten Pauschalreisen wurden angeboten, und die Flughäfen füllten sich mit Menschen, die ihren ersten Flug wagten. Der New Yorker Flughafen La Guardia gab stolz bekannt, daß er mit einer Zahl von 6,5 Millionen Passagieren pro Jahr rechne.

Die Autoindustrie fertigte eine größere Auswahl an Fahrzeugen als je zuvor. Vom geschwungenen Mercedes bis zum Heinkel Kabinenroller gab es einfach alles. Detroit produzierte eine enorme Bandbreite großer, schimmernder Limousinen. VW-Käfer rollten von deutschen Fertigungsstraßen. In Großbritannien entwarf Alec Issigonis den neuen Mini, und eine autobegeisterte konservative Regierung baute die ersten britischen Autobahnen.

Les transports connurent un nouvel âge d'or. De grands paquebots parcouraient toujours les océans du monde entier, offrant aux riches oisifs de luxueuses croisières. Mis à la mer en mai 1952, le SS *United States* décrocha le Ruban bleu deux mois plus tard, après sa traversée de l'Atlantique en un temps record – 3 jours, 10 heures et 40 minutes.

Quant au nouveau Bœing 707, il faisait beaucoup mieux. Ce jumbo, le premier de la série, pouvait voler à 960 km/heure avec 189 passagers à son bord. Il ouvrit l'ère des vacances organisées. Les aéroports se remplirent de voyageurs qui prenaient l'avion pour la première fois. L'aéroport de La Guardia à New York annonça avec un certain effroi qu'il devait s'attendre à 6,5 millions de visiteurs par an.

Pour les automobilistes, il y avait plus de choix que jamais, de la Mercedes à porte papillon à la petite voiture de Heinkel. A Detroit, Ford offrait une incroyable diversité de berlines aussi gigantesques qu'étincelantes. En Allemagne, Volkswagen produisait des coccinelles en série et, en Angleterre, Alec Issigonis créait la nouvelle Mini tandis qu'un gouvernement conservateur, fanatique de la voiture, faisait construire les premières autoroutes de Grande-Bretagne.

2 February 1952. The world's first passenger jet aircraft taxis onto the runway at Heathrow Airport. The De Havilland *Comet* had a chequered history. Metal fatigue led to a series of crashes, and when a strengthened version was introduced later in the Fifties, other jets had overtaken her.

2. Februar 1952. Das erste Passagierflugzeug mit Düsenantrieb rollt auf die Startbahn des Flughafens Heathrow. Die De Havilland *Comet* hatte eine bewegte Vergangenheit. Metallermüdung führte zu einer Reihe von Flugzeugabstürzen, und als einige Jahre später eine verbesserte Version eingeführt wurde, hatten andere Düsenflugzeuge ihr bereits den Rang abgelaufen.

2 février 1952. Le premier avion à réaction pour passagers roule doucement vers la piste de décollage de l'aéroport de Heathrow. Le *Comet* de De Havilland connut des hauts et des bas. Une fatigue du métal avait déjà causé plusieurs accidents. Quand un métal plus résistant fut enfin trouvé plus tard dans les années cinquante, d'autres avions avaient pris sa place.

February 1952. The streamlined hull of the SS *United States*. The ship was 990 feet long, and could cruise at 35 knots.

Februar 1952. Die stromlinienförmige SS *United States*. Das Schiff war mehr als 300 Meter lang und erreichte eine Reisegeschwindigkeit von 35 Knoten.

Février 1952. La coque aérodynamique du paquebot USS *United States*. Il mesurait plus de 300 mètres de long et pouvait atteindre une vitesse de croisière de 35 nœuds.

June 1950. The
largest airliner in the
world – the Bristol
Brabazon – at
Heathrow.

Juni 1950. Das
größte Verkehrs-
flugzeug der Welt –
die Bristol *Braba-
zon* – in Heathrow.

Juin 1950. Le plus
grand avion de ligne
du monde – le
Brabazon de Bristol
– à Heathrow.

Rule, Britannia! The aircraft carrier HMS *Ark Royal* glides down the slipway, 3 May 1950.

Es lebe Britannia! Der Flugzeugträger HMS *Ark Royal* gleitet die Helling hinab, 3. Mai 1950.

Vive Britannia! Le porte-avions HMS *Ark Royal* glisse à la mer, 3 mai 1950.

June 1951. The Saunders-Roe A1 jet flying boat is towed past Westminster, to be moored on the South Bank as part of the Festival of Britain.

Juni 1951. Dieses Saunders-Roe A1 Düsenflugboot wird im Schlepptau an Westminster vorbeigezogen und für die Dauer des Festival of Britain am Südufer der Themse vertäut.

Juin 1951. L'hydravion Saunders-Roe A1 est remorqué devant Westminster vers la rive Sud jusqu'au Festival of Britain.

BMW's 250 cc single-cylinder Isetta, at the International Motor Show in Earl's Court, London, October 1955. Unlike most other bubble cars, this Isetta had four wheels. A cross between a scooter and a baby car, bubble cars enjoyed only a short period of popularity.

Die Isetta von BMW mit Einzylindermotor und 250 ccm auf der Internationalen Automobil-ausstellung in Earl's Court, London, Oktober 1955. Im Gegensatz zu den meisten anderen Kabinenrollern besaß diese Isetta vier Räder. Als Mittelding zwischen einem Motorroller und einem Kleinwagen waren Kabinenroller nur eine kurze Zeit lang populär.

Le modèle Isetta à un cylindre et 250 cc de BMW au Salon de l'Auto à Earl's Court, Londres, octobre 1955. Contrairement aux autres petites voitures, cette Isetta avait quatre roues. La popularité de ces petites voitures, mi-scooter, mi-voiture pour enfant, ne dura pas longtemps.

The 1959 Austin Seven, with the amount of luggage it was reputed to hold. The 'Seven' was a sister car to the Morris Mini, but it never became as popular, and production ceased early in the Sixties.

Der 1959er Austin Seven sollte all die Dinge und Personen unterbringen können. Der „Seven", der kleine Bruder des Morris Mini, erreichte jedoch nie dessen Popularität, so daß seine Produktion in den frühen sechziger Jahren eingestellt wurde.

L'Austin seven de 1959 et tous les bagages qu'elle était censée pouvoir contenir. La « Seven » , petite sœur de la Mini de Morris, ne connut pas le même succès et sa production cessa au début des années soixante.

March 1959. Volkswagen cars and vans await loading onto the
transport ship *Fidelio* in Bremen Harbour, Germany. They were
destined for the United States, a vital market for most European car
manufacturers in the Fifties.

März 1959. VW-Busse und Käfer warten im Bremer Hafen, um auf
das Transportschiff *Fidelio* verladen zu werden. Sie waren für den
amerikanischen Markt bestimmt, der in den fünfziger Jahren für die
meisten europäischen Autohersteller lebenswichtig war.

Mars 1959. Chargement de fourgons et de voitures Volkswagen à
bord du *Fidelio*, port de Brême, Allemagne. Ces véhicules étaient
destinés au marché américain, vital dans les années cinquante pour la
majorité des fabricants de voiture européens.

Volkswagen 'Beetles' lined up outside a German factory in 1956. Owners had great affection for these cars, and would salute fellow owners as they passed on the roads.

Nagelneue „Käfer" vor einem deutschen VW-Werk, 1956. Käfer-Besitzer liebten ihre Autos im allgemeinen sehr und grüßten andere Käfer-Fahrer, wenn sie ihnen im Straßenverkehr begegneten.

Les « Coccinelles » en rang devant l'usine Volkswagen, Allemagne, 1956. Les propriétaires de ces modèles débordaient d'affection pour leur voiture et ne manquaient jamais de saluer leurs « homologues » quand ils se croisaient sur la route.

Cars queue at the entrance to the Olympic drive-in cinema in
California, April 1951. Drive-in theatres often had poor picture
definition and inadequate sound reproduction, but few couples went
there to see the films anyway.

Autoschlangen vor dem Autokino Olympic in Kalifornien, April 1951.
Autokinos besaßen zwar häufig eine schlechte Bild- und eine
mangelhafte Tonqualität, doch fuhr sowieso kaum ein junges Paar
dorthin, nur um einen Film zu sehen.

Des voitures font la queue pour entrer au cinéma drive-in en
Californie, avril 1951. La qualité du son et de l'image de ces cinémas
était souvent médiocre mais, de toute façon, peu de couples y allaient
pour voir le film.

The American Dream of the Fifties. A smooth limousine, a straight empty road, a distant horizon and cheap gas. This is the motorway across the Bonneville Salt Flats, Utah, November 1950.

Der Amerikanische Traum der fünfziger Jahre. Eine elegante Limousine, eine schnurgerade, leere Straße, ein scheinbar endloser Horizont und preiswertes Benzin. Dieser Highway führte durch die Salzebenen von Bonneville im US-Staat Utah, November 1950.

Le rêve américain des années cinquante. Une limousine confortable, une route droite et déserte, un horizon lointain et de l'essence bon marché. Cette route traverse Bonneville Salt Flats, Utah, novembre 1950.

The Italian Dream of the Fifties. A noble city, a sunny day, and plenty of beautiful women to pursue on a sporty new scooter. In this case, the two Romeos are riding Vespas, and the year is 1950.

Der italienische Traum der fünfziger Jahre. Eine prächtige Stadt, ein sonniger Tag und zahllose schöne Frauen, denen man auf dem neuen Motorroller nachjagen konnte. Die beiden Romeos auf dieser Aufnahme aus dem Jahre 1950 waren auf Vespas unterwegs.

Le rêve italien des années cinquante. Une ville magnifique, du soleil et beaucoup de belles femmes à poursuivre à bord d'un scooter neuf à l'allure sportive. On est en 1950 et ces deux Roméo conduisent des Vespas.

'A typical shopping trip in 1955'. However, the 'housewife' is model Shirley Worthington and the outfit hardly seems suitable for shopping or riding a scooter.

„Eine typische Einkaufsfahrt für das Jahr 1955". Doch die „Hausfrau" ist ein Mannequin, Shirley Worthington, und ihre Kleidung scheint kaum passend zu sein, um einkaufen zu gehen oder Roller zu fahren.

« Un lèche-vitrines typique en 1955 ». Mais, comme nous le révèle sa tenue peu adaptée pour faire des courses ou conduire un scooter, la « ménagère » est en réalité le mannequin Shirley Worthington.

Car of the future. This is the shell of the French Simca Fulgar, designed for
the year 2000, though the picture was taken in December 1958. The car was
to be atomic-powered and guided by radar. It had only two wheels, balanced
by gyroscopes at speeds of up to 90mph.

Ein Auto der Zukunft. Diese Aufnahme vom Dezember 1958 zeigt die
Karosserie des französischen Simca Fulgar, der für das Jahr 2000 entworfen
wurde. Das Auto sollte Nuklearantrieb und ein Radarleitsystem besitzen. Es
fuhr auf nur zwei Rädern, die bei Geschwindigkeiten von bis zu 145 km/h von
Kreiseln ausbalanciert wurden.

La voiture du futur. Coque de la Simca française Fulgar conçue pour l'an
2000, photographiée en décembre 1958. Elle devait être alimentée en énergie
nucléaire et guidée au radar. Maintenue en équilibre sur ses deux roues par
des gyroscopes, elle pouvait atteindre la vitesse de 145 km/heure.

Ship of the present. The Saunders-Roe SRN-1 hovercraft
about to undergo its sea trials in 1959. Invented by
Christopher Cockerell, the hovercraft was one of the
'futuristic' designs of the 1950s that did succeed.

Ein Schiff der Gegenwart. Das Saunders-Roe SRN-1
Luftkissenboot vor seiner Testfahrt zu Wasser, 1959. Diese
Erfindung von Christopher Cockerell war eines der
„futuristischen" Konzepte, denen Erfolg vergönnt war.

Le bateau du présent. L'aéroglisseur Saunders-Roe SRN-1
sur le point d'entamer une série d'essais en mer, 1959.
Inventé par Christopher Cockerell, l'aéroglisseur fut l'un
des designs « futuristes » des années cinquante à avoir
du succès.

13. Sport
Sport
Le sport

August 1954. The Czechoslovakian athlete Emil Zátopek, on the way
to winning the 10,000 metres in Bern, Switzerland. Zátopek had a
curious, laboured running style, but he broke 13 middle-distance
running records between 1948 and 1954.

August 1954. Der tschechoslowakische Athlet Emil Zátopek bei
seinem Siegeslauf über 10.000 Meter in Bern, Schweiz. Zátopek besaß
zwar einen eigentümlichen, angestrengten Laufstil, stellte aber 13
Mittelstreckenrekorde zwischen 1948 und 1954 auf.

Août 1954. L'athlète tchécoslovaque Emil Zátopek sur le chemin de la
victoire du 10 000 mètres, Berne, Suisse. Zátopek avait une façon de
courir surprenante par son style peu aérien, ce qui ne l'empêcha pas de
battre 13 records de course de distance moyenne entre 1948 et 1954.

13. Sport
Sport
Le sport

Two sporting 'firsts' stand out in the Fifties. On a grey May evening in Oxford in 1954, Roger Bannister became the first athlete to run a mile in under four minutes. Three years earlier, thousands of miles away, Althea Gibson became the first black tennis player to compete in the US Championships. Bannister became a doctor. Gibson became a champion.

Emil Zátopek took three gold medals at the Helsinki Olympics in 1952. His wife, Dana, broke the Olympic record for the Women's Javelin. Britain won a single gold medal 15 minutes before the closing ceremony, thanks to a horse called Foxhunter.

Other heroes left the scene. Mike Hawthorn, second only to Juan Fangio as a racing driver throughout the decade, died in a car crash in 1959. Maureen Connolly, better known as Little Mo, won the US tennis title from 1951 to 1953, and the Wimbledon title from 1952 to 1954. Then she broke her leg in a riding accident and had to give up the game she loved. Rocky Marciano punched his way to the World Heavyweight crown, but quit fighting in 1956. 'Barring poverty,' he said, 'the ring has seen the last of me.'

And on 6 February 1958, seven of Manchester United's Busby Babes were killed in a plane crash at Munich Airport.

Zwei Ereignisse gingen in den fünfziger Jahren als Novum in die Geschichte des Sports ein. An einem trüben Maiabend im Jahre 1954 lief Roger Bannister in Oxford als erster Athlet eine Meile in weniger als vier Minuten. Drei Jahre zuvor und Tausende von Kilometern entfernt nahm Althea Gibson als erste schwarze Tennisspielerin an den amerikanischen Meisterschaften teil. Bannister wurde später Arzt und Gibson Meisterin.

Emil Zátopek errang 1952 drei Goldmedaillen bei den Olympischen Spielen von Helsinki. Seine Ehefrau Dana erzielte einen neuen olympischen Rekord im Speerwurf der rauen. Großbritannien gewann schließlich eine einzige Goldmedaille, 15 Minuten vor Beginn der Schlußzeremonie der Olympiade, dank eines Pferdes namens Foxhunter.

Andere Idole verlor die Sportwelt. Mike Hawthorn, als Rennfahrer das ganze Jahrzehnt lang nur von Juan Fangio übertroffen, kam bei einem Autounfall 1959 ums Leben. Maureen Connolly, besser bekannt als „Little Mo", gewann sowohl die amerikanischen Meisterschaften von 1951 bis 1953 als auch Wimbledon von 1952 bis 1954. Dann brach sie sich bei einem Reitunfall ein Bein und mußte den Sport, den sie so sehr liebte, aufgeben. Rocky Marciano boxte sich zum Weltmeister im Schwergewicht empor, bis er 1956 das Boxen aufgab. „Falls mich die Armut nicht dazu treibt, steige ich nie wieder in den Ring", erkündete er.

Und am 6. Februar 1958 verloren sieben Spieler von Manchester United bei einem Flugzeugunglück auf dem Münchener Flughafen ihr Leben.

Deux « premières » marquent le sport des années cinquante. En 1954 à Oxford, par une soirée maussade de mai, Roger Bannister fut le premier athlète à courir le mile en moins de quatre minutes. Trois ans plus tôt, à des milliers de kilomètres de là, Althea Gibson était devenu le premier joueur de tennis noir à participer au championnat des Etats-Unis. Plus tard, Bannister devint médecin et Gibson un champion.

Emil Zátopek remporta trois médailles d'or aux Jeux olympiques d'Helsinki en 1952. Sa femme, Dana, battit le record olympique du javelot dames. Quant à la Grande-Bretagne, elle gagna une seule médaille d'or, quinze minutes avant la cérémonie de clôture, grâce à un cheval nommé Foxhunter.

D'autres héros quittèrent la scène. Mike Hawthorn, le plus grand pilote de course de la décennie après Juan Fangio, mourut dans un accident de voiture en 1959. La joueuse de tennis Maureen Connolly, mieux connue sous le nom de Little Mo, remporta l'Open U. S. de 1951 à 1953 et Wimbledon de 1952 à 1954. Puis, elle se cassa la jambe dans un accident de cheval et dut renoncer au sport qu'elle aimait tant. Le boxeur Rocky Marciano décrocha le titre de champion du monde des poids lourds mais abandonna la boxe en 1956. « Je ne remonterai plus sur le ring à moins d'être complètement fauché », déclara-t-il.

Enfin, le 6 février 1958, sept joueurs du Manchester United trouvèrent la mort dans l'avion qui s'écrasa à l'aéroport de Munich.

British racing driver Stirling Moss, shortly after winning the Italian Mille Miglia, May 1955.

Der britische Rennfahrer Stirling Moss nach seinem Sieg im italienischen Mille-Miglia-Rennen, Mai 1955.

Le pilote de course britannique Stirling Moss juste après sa victoire à la course de Mille Miglia en Italie, mai 1955.

6 May 1954. An exhausted Roger Bannister, just after he had run a mile in 3 minutes 59.4 seconds at Iffley Road, Oxford.

6. Mai 1954. Der erschöpfte Roger Bannister, nachdem er eine Meile in 3 Minuten und 59,4 Sekunden gelaufen war in der Iffley Road, Oxford.

6 mai 1954. Un Roger Bannister épuisé après avoir couru un mile en 3 minutes 59,4 secondes à Iffley Road, Oxford.

Alf Ramsay, captain
of Tottenham
Hotspur, training in
Epping Forest,
1952. From 1963 to
1974 he was
manager of the
England team.

Alf Ramsay,
Mannschaftskapitän
von Tottenham
Hotspurs, trainiert
in Epping Forest,
1952. Von 1963 bis
1974 war er der
Trainer der
englischen
Nationalmannschaft.

Alf Ramsay,
capitaine du club de
Tottenham Hotspur,
s'entraîne à Epping
Forest, 1952.
Il fut de 1963 à
1974 le dirigeant de
l'équipe
d'Angleterre.

October 1951. In the days of long shorts and heavy leather footballs, Butler of Portsmouth (left) and McDonald of Fulham wrestle for possession at the Craven Cottage ground in West London.

Oktober 1951. Die Shorts waren noch lang und der Fußball aus schwerem Leder, Butler von Portsmouth (links) und McDonald von Fulham kämpfen um den Ballbesitz auf dem Fußballplatz Craven Cottage, West-London.

Octobre 1951. A l'époque des shorts longs et des balles en cuir épais, Butler de Portsmouth (à gauche) et McDonald de Fulham se disputent le terrain sur le stade de Craven Cottage, à l'ouest de Londres.

5 February 1958. The Manchester United team line up on the pitch
at Belgrade before the kick-off in their European Cup quarter-final
match against Red Star. The result was a 3-3 draw. The following
day they began their journey back to Manchester.

5. Februar 1958. Das Team von Manchester United in Aufstellung
auf dem Fußballfeld in Belgrad vor dem Anstoß ihres
Viertelfinalspiels um den Europapokal gegen die Red Stars. Das
Spiel endete 3:3. Am Tag darauf traten die Briten ihre Heimreise
nach Manchester an.

Le 5 février 1958. L'équipe du Manchester United alignée sur le
terrain à Belgrade, avant le coup d'envoi de la quart de finale contre
le Red Star comptant pour la Coupe d'Europe. Ce fut un match nul
à trois partout. L'équipe devait regagner Manchester le lendemain.

Just after three o'clock the following afternoon, the Elizabethan airliner in which the team was travelling crashed at the end of the runway. Seven of the most gifted young players in football were killed.

Am folgenden Tag, kurz nach drei Uhr, zerschellte die Maschine, in der die Mannschaft reiste, am Ende der Rollbahn. Sieben der talentiertesten jungen Fußballer kamen ums Leben.

Le lendemain, peu après 15 heures, l'avion qui transportait l'équipe s'écrasa en bout de piste. Sept joueurs, parmi les plus talentueux du monde du football, étaient tués.

August 1954. Members of the West Ham football team practise
dribbling between sets of posts as part of their pre-season warm-up.

August 1954. Spieler der Fußballmannschaft von West Ham bereiten
sich mit einem Dribbeltraining zwischen Slalompfosten auf
die bevorstehende Saison vor.

Août 1954. Des joueurs de l'équipe de football de West Ham
s'entraînent à dribbler entre les poteaux. Cet exercice faisait partie
de l'entraînement avant l'ouverture de la saison.

Polo for the masses… Members of the Norwegian Paragon team show their skills in the saddle during a game of bicycle polo in 1952.

Polo für das Volk… Sportler der norwegischen Paragon-Mannschaft demonstrieren ihr Können im Sattel während eines Fahrrad-Polospiels, 1952.

Polo du peuple… Des joueurs de l'équipe Paragon de Norvège font une démonstration de leur bonne tenue en selle lors d'un jeu de polo à bicyclette, 1952.

At the Olympic Pool, Helsinki, July 1952. French swimmer Jean
Boiteux is helping his father from the water. When Boiteux won the
400 metres freestyle, his father became so excited that he fell in.

Im olympischen Becken, Helsinki, Juli 1952. Der französische
Schwimmer Jean Boiteux hilft seinem Vater aus dem Wasser.
Der Sieg seines Sohnes über 400 Meter Freistil versetzte Boiteux
Senior in solche Begeisterung, daß er ins Becken fiel.

Piscine olympique, Helsinki, juillet 1952. Le nageur français Jean
Boiteux aide son père à sortir de l'eau. Ne pouvant contenir
son enthousiasme après la victoire de son fils au 400 mètres libre, il était
tombé dans le bassin.

Tarzan takes to the water in 1950. Johnny Weissmuller was
born in Romania in 1903, but won five Olympic gold medals
for the United States, his adopted home. He also starred in 19
Tarzan films.

Tarzan am Start, 1950. Johnny Weissmuller, 1903 in Rumänien
geboren, gewann fünfmal olympisches Gold für seine Wahl-
heimat Amerika. Er spielte außerdem die Titelrolle in
19 Tarzan-Filmen.

Tarzan prêt à plonger, 1950. Né en Roumanie en 1903, Johnny
Weissmuller remporta 5 médailles d'or olympiques pour les
Etats-Unis, son pays d'adoption, et tourna 19 films de Tarzan.

June 1950. Gertrude 'Gorgeous Gussie' Moran parades her tennis bloomers, designed for her by Pierre Balmain for the Wimbledon Championships.

Juni 1959. Gertrude Moran, die „hinreißende Gussie", führt die Tennishöschen vor, die Pierre Balmain anläßlich des Wimbledon-Turniers für sie kreierte hatte.

Juin 1950. Gertrude Moran, surnommée « la belle Gussie » présente ses culottes de tennis bouffantes, créées pour elle par Pierre Balmain pour le tournoi de Wimbledon.

Members of the Brentford football team enjoy a training session at a local swimming bath in London, January 1950. It was part of their build-up to a Cup match against Chelsea. (Left to right) Goodwin, Greenwood, Sherin, Jeffries and Dr O'Flanigan.

Spieler der Fußballmannschaft von Brentford beim Training in einer Londoner Badeanstalt, Januar 1950. Sie bereiteten sich auf ein Pokalspiel gegen Chelsea vor. (Von links nach rechts) Goodwin, Greenwood, Sherin, Jeffries und Dr. O'Flanigan.

Des joueurs de l'équipe de foot de Brentford s'amusent pendant leur entraînement à la piscine du coin, Londres, janvier 1950. Cela faisait partie de leur mise en forme avant le match contre Chelsea comptant pour la Coupe. (De gauche à droite) Goodwin, Greenwood, Sherin, Jeffries et le Dr. O'Flanigan.

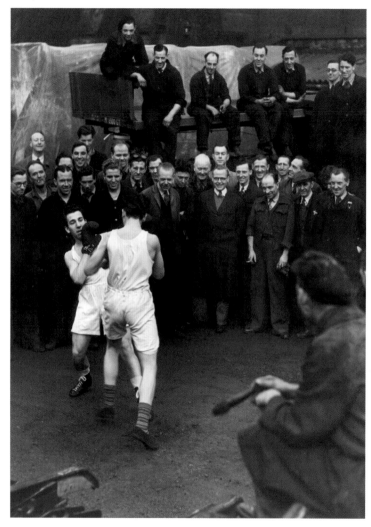

Amateur hopefuls. Two apprentices – James Jeffries (left) and John Ince (right) spar together during the British Railways National Boxing Championships, Kentish Town, London, 1950.

Amateur-Hoffnungen. Zwei Lehrlinge – James Jeffries (links) und John Ince (rechts) – beim Sparring während der Nationalen Boxmeisterschaften der Britischen Eisenbahn, Kentish Town, London, 1950.

Jeunes espoirs amateurs. Deux apprentis – James Jeffries (à gauche) et John Ince (à droite) livrent un combat amical comptant pour le Championnat national de boxe des cheminots, Kentish Town, Londres, 1950.

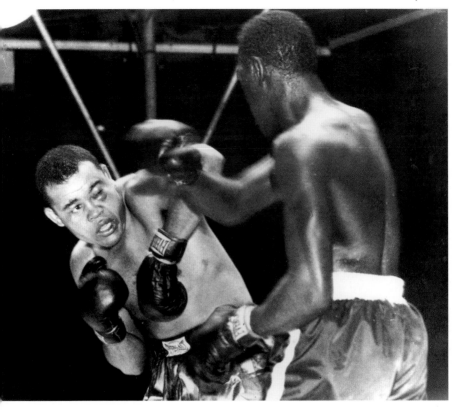

Professional rivals. Joe Louis (left) makes an unsuccessful attempt to win back his World Heavyweight crown from Ezzard Charles at the Yankee Stadium, New York, 29 September 1950.

Professionelle Rivalen. Joe Louis (links) unternimmt einen vergeblichen Versuch, Ezzard Charles den Weltmeistertitel im Schwergewicht im Yankee Stadion, New York, abzunehmen, 29. September 1950.

Adversaires professionnels. Joe Louis (à gauche) tente en vain de reconquérir son titre de champion du monde des poids lourds face à Ezzard Charles au Yankee Stadium, New York, 29 septembre 1950.

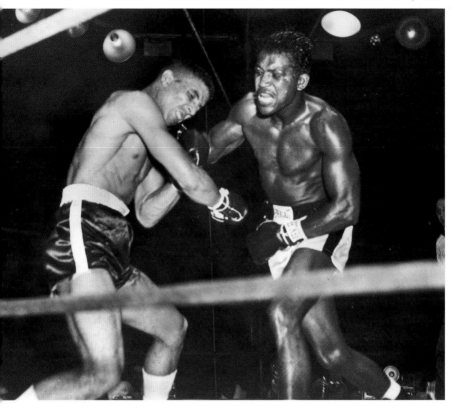

The American boxer Sugar Ray Robinson (left) in Paris, 7 July 1951. Three days later Robinson lost his Middleweight crown to the British fighter, Randolph Turpin. Turpin (above) buckles under a blow from Robinson during the return match at the Polo Ground, New York, 12 September 1951.

Der amerikanische Boxer Sugar Ray Robinson (links) in Paris, 7. Juli 1951. Drei Tage später verlor Robinson seinen Meistertitel im Mittelgewicht an den britischen Boxer Randolph Turpin. Turpin (oben) muß während des Revanchekampfes im Polo Ground, New York, einen schweren Schlag von Robinson einstecken, 12. September 1951.

Le boxeur américain Sugar Ray Robinson (à gauche) à Paris, 7 juillet 1951. Trois jours plus tard, Robinson perdait son titre, catégorie poids moyens, au profit du pugiliste britannique, Randolph Turpin. Turpin (ci-dessus) flanche sous un coup de Robinson au cours du match retour au Polo Ground, New York, 12 septembre 1951.

November 1954. The noble art of self-defence. (Left to right) Jim and Henry Cooper, professional boxing twins from London. Henry later became a contender for the World Heavyweight title, and even succeeded in flooring Muhammed Ali.

November 1954. Die edle Kunst der Selbstverteidigung. (Von links nach rechts) Jim und Henry Cooper, Zwillinge und Profiboxer aus London. Henry kämpfte später um den Weltmeistertitel im Schwergewicht. Es gelang ihm sogar, Mohammed Ali niederzustrecken.

Novembre 1954. Le noble art de l'auto-défense. (De gauche à droite) Jim et Henry Cooper, jumeaux et boxeurs professionnels de Londres. Henry fut, plus tard, candidat au titre de champion du monde poids moyens et réussit même à mettre Mohammed Ali au tapis.

February 1952. The ignoble art of gangland attack. (Left to right) Ronnie and Reggie Kray, who began their careers in the boxing ring, but later became ruthlessly violent leaders of an East End gang in London.

Februar 1952. Die unehrenhafte Kunst des Unterwelt-Angriffs. (Von links nach rechts) Ronnie und Reggie Kray begannen ihre Karriere zwar im Boxring, später aber erlangten sie zweifelhaften Ruhm als gewalttätige Anführer einer Londoner East-End-Gang.

Février 1952. L'ignoble art du règlement de comptes. (De gauche à droite) Ronnie et Reggie Kray firent leurs débuts sur le ring avant de devenir les chefs impitoyables et violents d'un gang de l'East End à Londres.

Le Mans, 11 June 1955 – the worst crash in the history of motor racing. During the 24-hour race, a Mercedes spun out of control into the crowd, and exploded. 84 people were killed and over a 100 injured.

Le Mans, 11. Juni 1955 – der verheerendste Unfall in der Geschichte des Motorsports. Ein Mercedes geriet während des 24-Stunden-Rennens ins Schleudern, raste in die Zuschauermenge und explodierte. Das Unglück forderte 84 Tote und über 100 Verletzte.

Le Mans, 11 juin 1955 – le plus grave accident de l'histoire de la course automobile. Au cours des « 24 heures », une Mercedes hors de contrôle fonça dans la foule et explosa. 84 personnes furent tuées et plus d'une centaine d'autres blessées.

The Argentinian racing driver Juan Manuel Fangio with his wife at Silverstone, February 1954. Fangio was world champion from 1954 to 1957.

Der argentinische Rennfahrer Juan Manuel Fangio mit seiner Ehefrau in Silverstone, Februar 1954. Fangio war von 1954 bis 1957 Weltmeister.

Le pilote argentin Juan Manuel Fangio et sa femme à Silverstone, février 1954. Fangio fut champion du monde de 1954 à 1957.

June 1958.
The Italian cyclist
Brandolini gets a
'flying saddle' repair
from the Bianchi
team support car
during the Tour
of Italy.

Juni 1958.
Der italienische
Radrennfahrer
Brandolini erhält
eine „fliegende"
Sattelreparatur vom
Betreuungswagen
des Bianchi-Teams
während der
All'Italia.

Juin 1958.
Le cycliste italien
Brandolini se fait
réparer sa selle « en
vol » par un membre
de l'équipe tech-
nique qui le suit
dans une Bianchi
pendant le
Tour d'Italie.

1959. A luckless rider flies from the saddle of his fallen steed during the Virginia Water Steeplechase at Windsor, near London.

1959. Ein Jockey wird beim Virginia-Water-Hindernisrennen in Windsor bei London aus dem Sattel seines stürzenden Pferdes geschleudert.

1959. Un jockey malchanceux tombe cul par-dessus tête de son cheval tombé pendant la course du Virginia Water Steeplechase à Windsor, près de Londres.

14. Children
Kinder
Les enfants

A street ambush, August 1954. These boys' heroes would have been Roy Rogers and Gene Autry, or, if they were devotees of the Saturday morning cinema club, the Lone Ranger. Only those with access to a television set knew of Hopalong Cassidy.

Überfall an der Straßenecke, August 1954. Die Idole dieser Jungen waren vermutlich Roy Rogers und Gene Autry oder, falls sie am Samstagmorgen regelmäßig das Kino besuchten, Lone Ranger. Nur wer damals schon Zugang zu einem Fernseher hatte, kannte auch Hopalong Cassidy.

Embuscade au coin d'une rue, août 1954. Ces garçons avaient pour héros Roy Rogers et Gene Autry ou, s'ils allaient à la séance du samedi matin du club de cinéma, Lone Ranger. Seuls les enfants dont les parents avaient un poste de télévision connaissaient Hopalong Cassidy.

14. Children
Kinder
Les enfants

The Fifties child was uncomfortably poised between the immediate post-war idealism of the late Forties, and the burgeoning freedom of the Swinging Sixties. Life for most children was still tough. Corporal punishment flourished at home and school, and many regarded it as a mercy that their formal education was over by the time they were 14 or 15.

The toy famine of the Forties came to an end as factories were rebuilt and rejigged to produce aircraft, trains and cars. The old favourites were still popular – marbles, tops and hoops – but a market was rapidly being created for more sophisticated and expensive playthings. Ray guns were all the rage as comic strip heroes entered the Space Age, and there was much demand for spy kits, as befitted the Cold War.

City children lost their best playgrounds as the number of bomb sites dwindled. But many streets were still traffic-free enough to play on. Life was good, and the combination of a sunny day and a vivid imagination transported children in their thousands to the Wild West, the Middle Ages, the high seas or the Roman Empire.

There was also the hope that the United Nations might be able to do something about the vast sections of the world where 'childhood' barely existed.

Das Kind der fünfziger Jahre wuchs zwischen dem Nachkriegsidealismus der späten vierziger Jahre und der bereits keimenden Freiheit der Swinging Sixties auf. Für die meisten Kinder war das Leben noch immer hart. Die Prügelstrafe war im Elternhaus ebenso wie in der Schule üblich, und viele Heranwachsende betrachteten es als einen Segen, daß ihre Schulpflicht mit 14 oder 15 Jahren endete.

Die Spielzeugnot der vierziger Jahre war endgültig vorüber. Die Fabriken wurden wieder aufgebaut und umstrukturiert, um Flugzeuge, Eisenbahnen und Autos zu produzieren. Die alten Favoriten – Murmeln, Kreisel und Reifen – hatten zwar nichts an Beliebtheit eingebüßt och im Handumdrehen entstand ein zusätzlicher neuer Markt für anspruchsvollere und eurere Spielsachen. Strahlenpistolen waren der letzte Schrei, als Comic-Helden begannen, en Weltraum zu erobern, und auch die Nachfrage nach Spionspielen und -zubehör war groß entsprechend der Zeit des Kalten Krieges.

Stadtkinder mußten ihre besten Spielplätze aufgeben, denn Trümmergrundstücke wurden ar. Doch es gab kaum Verkehr, so daß auf den Straßen gespielt werden konnte. Das Leben ar schön, und an einem sonnigen Tag brachen Tausende von Kinder in ihre Phantasiewelt uf, in den Wilden Westen, ins Mittelalter, auf Hohe See oder ins römische Weltreich.

Man setzte große Hoffnungen auf die Vereinten Nationen, sich für Kinder in den ereichen der Welt einzusetzen, in denen die Kindheit mißachtet wurde.

es enfants des années cinquante étaient pris en sandwich entre l'idéalisme de l'après-guerre ui avait marqué la fin des années quarante et une liberté nouvelle qui s'affirmerait dans les sixties ». Mais, pour la majorité d'entre eux, la vie était encore dure. La punition corporelle tait courante à la maison comme à l'école et les parents plutôt satisfaits que l'école bligatoire se termine autour de 14 ou 15 ans.

Les jouets, qui avaient cruellement fait défaut dans les années quarante, réapparurent. Les sines étaient reconstruites et produisaient de nouveau des avions, des trains et des voitures. es grands classiques, comme les billes et le croquet, connaissaient toujours autant de succès. ourtant, un marché de jouets plus sophistiqués et plus chers était en train de voir le jour. Les usils à rayon laser des héros de bandes dessinées, voyageant dans l'espace. faisaient fureur. es coffrets d'espions en herbe étaient eux aussi fort prisés – en phase avec la guerre froide.

Avec la disparition progressive des sites dévastés par les bombes, les petits citadins erdaient leurs meilleurs terrains de jeux. Heureusement, il y avait peu de circulation et il tait encore possible de jouer dans la rue. La vie était agréable : un jour ensoleillé et une magination débordante suffisaient à des milliers d'enfants pour se transporter au Far West, à 'époque du Moyen-Age ou de l'Empire romain ou s'imaginer partis à la conquête des mers.

Enfin, on nourrissait l'espoir que les Nations unies pourraient intervenir dans les nnombrables régions du monde où l'enfance était bafouée.

Live show. A young boy gazes in fascination
at a tank of fish at Hexham market in the
North of England, October 1950.

Live-Show. Ein Junge betrachtet fasziniert ein
Aquarium auf dem Marktplatz von Hexham
in Nordengland, Oktober 1950.

Spectacle. Ce petit garçon est fasciné par un
aquarium exposé au marché d'Hexham, nord
de l'Angleterre, octobre 1950.

June 1950. Young Malcolm Graves watches his favourite television programme at home in Harrow, London. The programme was *Muffin the Mule*, a puppet show of some charm and little skill. The Graves family may well have been among the first to own a TV set in Harrow.

Juni 1950. Der kleine Malcolm Graves sieht sein Lieblingsprogramm zu Hause in Harrow, London. Die Sendung hieß *Muffin, das Maultier*, ein Puppentheater mit einigem Charme und geringer Kunstfertigkeit. Der Fernseher der Familie Graves gehörte möglicherweise zu den ersten Geräten in Harrow.

Juin 1950. Le petit Malcolm Graves regarde son émission favorite à la maison, Harrow, Londres. L'émission s'appelait *Muffin the Mule*, un spectacle de marionnettes gentillet et rudimentaire. Il est fort possible que les Graves aient été les premiers dans le quartier d'Harrow à posséder un téléviseur.

October 1951. The deprivations of the poor. A
barefoot girl sits with her classmates in a school in
Lancashire, northern England.

Oktober 1951. Die Entbehrungen der Armen. Ein
barfüßiges Mädchen sitzt mit ihren Klassenkameraden
in einer Schule in Lancashire, Nordengland.

Octobre 1951. Les privations des pauvres. Une
fillette, pieds nus, assise en classe dans une école du
Lancashire, nord de l'Angleterre.

October 1951. The depravities of the rich. Three girls share a cigarette on their way back to boarding school by train. They have almost certainly just said goodbye to their parents, who know nothing of this secret vice.

Oktober 1951. Die Laster der Wohlhabenden. Drei Internatsschülerinnen teilen sich eine Zigarette auf der Bahnfahrt zurück in die Schule. Ihre Eltern, von denen sie sich eben erst verabschiedet hatten, wußten wohl nichts von diesem geheimen Laster.

Octobre 1951. Les débauches des riches. Ces trois filles partagent une cigarette dans le train les ramenant au pensionnat. Elles viennent certainement de dire au revoir à leurs parents, qui ignorent tout de ce vice secret.

July 1952. The soapbox Derby Day. A variety of vehicles make their way to the starting line i Leighton Buzzard, England.

Juli 1952. Der große Tag des Seifenkisten Rennens. Die unter schiedlichsten Fahr-zeuge gingen in Leighton Buzzard, England, an den Start.

Juillet 1952. Le Derby en caisse à savon. Des véhicule en tout genre se dirigent vers la ligne de départ à Leighton Buzzard, Angleterre

Children curl up in the luggage space of the Standard 8 car, a model
first brought out in 1953. For a while it was the cheapest four-door
saloon car in Britain, but it had a short production life.

Zwei Kinder amüsieren sich im Kofferraum eines Standard-8-Wagens,
ein Modell, das erstmals 1953 herausgebracht wurde. Eine Zeitlang
war dies die preiswerteste, viertürige britische Limousine, doch die
Produktion wurde sehr bald eingestellt.

Enfants blottis au fond du coffre de la Standard 8, un modèle
de voiture sorti pour la première fois en 1953. Elle fut pendant
quelque temps la berline à quatre portes la moins chère de Grande-
Bretagne mais sa production ne dura pas.

May 1952. Two schoolboys share the delights of an American comic. There were those who said that 'Yank Mags' should be banned from Britain on the grounds that they were too explicitly violent.

Mai 1952. Zwei Schulkinder lesen gemeinsam einen amerikanischen Comic. Mancherorts wurden Stimmen laut, „Yankee Magazine" in Großbritannien zu verbieten, da sie zuviel Gewalt enthielten.

Mai 1952. Deux écoliers lisent une bande dessinée américaine. Selon certains, les « journaux yankee » auraient dû être interdits en Grande-Bretagne, en raison de leur violence trop explicite.

November 1959. Two schoolboys play the time-honoured game of
'conkers' in Gravesend, Kent. At hand to see fair play is the Rev. R
Barrington of Milton Church.

November 1959. Zwei Schulkinder beim Austragen des traditionellen
Kastanien-Wettkampfes „Conkers" in Gravesend, Kent. Pfarrer R.
Barrington von der Milton Kirche überwacht strengen Auges die
Einhaltung der Regeln.

Novembre 1959. Deux écoliers jouent à un jeu appelé « Conkers »
consistant à casser le marron accroché au fil de l'adversaire,
Gravesend, Kent. Le révérend R. Barrington de l'église de Milton
s'assure du fair-play des participants.

A group of children play hopscotch in the street, April 1950. Children believed that treading on the line between two paving stones would bring bad luck: 'You will break your spine;' 'You will get your sums wrong;' 'You will marry a swine.'

Eine Gruppe von Kindern spielen Himmel und Hölle auf dem Bürgersteig, April 1950. Viele Kinder glaubten daran, daß ein Tritt auf die Linie zwischen zwei Pflastersteinen Unglück brachte: „Du wirst dir das Rückgrat brechen", „Du wirst dich in der Schule verrechnen" oder „Du wirst ein Schwein heiraten".

Un groupe d'enfants joue à la marelle dans la rue, avril 1950. Marcher sur la ligne qui séparait les pavés portait malchance: « Tu vas te casser le cou », « tu vas te tromper au calcul », « tu vas te marier avec un cochon », criaient les enfants au perdant.

April 1950. Two boys flick bottle tops along the pavement in a game they have probably devised themselves. The setting is Tiger Bay, one of the poorest districts of the Cardiff docklands.

April 1950. Zwei Jungen schnipsen Flaschenverschlüsse über den Bürgersteig, ein Spiel, dessen Regeln sie sich vermutlich selbst ausgedacht haben. Der Schauplatz ist Tiger Bay, einer der ärmsten Gegenden des Hafenviertels von Cardiff.

Avril 1950. Deux garçons lancent des capsules de bouteilles sur le trottoir, jeu qu'ils ont probablement inventé. La scène se déroule à Tiger Bay, l'un des quartiers les plus pauvres des docks de Cardiff.

The Battle of the
Little Coal Shute.
A young warrior
takes careful aim in
a street game, 1954.

Die Schlacht am
Kleinen Kohlen-
schacht. Ein junger
Krieger legt bei
einem Straßenspiel
vorsichtig an, 1954.

Les Cow-boys et
les Indiens. Jeu de
rue pour un jeune
guerrier qui met en
joue sa cible, 1954.

aunt of an urban
rzan, 1955. The
np-post is in a
reet that has been
ecially designated
a play area for
ildren.

eblingsplatz eines
adt-Tarzans, 1955.
e Straßenlaterne
eht in einer extra
r Kinder ausge-
esenen
pielstraße.

vocation d'un
rzan des villes,
955. Le lampadaire
t situé dans une
e spécialement
nçue pour servir
e terrain de jeux
x enfants.

October 1958. Pupils of the Mount Stewart Junior Mixed School, Middlesex. In the Fifties great emphasis was laid on the importance of physical education for young children, and every modern school had its own playing fields.

Oktober 1958. Schüler der koedukativen Mount-Stewart-Grundschule in Middlesex. In den fünfziger Jahren legte man großen Wert auf die Leibeserziehung der Kinder, und jede moderne Schule besaß einen eigenen Sportplatz.

Octobre 1958. Des élèves de l'école primaire mixte de Mount Stewart, Middlesex. Dans les années cinquante, on accorda beaucoup d'importance à l'éducation physique des jeunes enfants. Chaque école moderne disposait d'un terrain de sports.

The Famous Four. The Taylor Quads from Edmonton in London
bounce down the road on their pogo sticks, 1958. Quadruplets
were a rare phenomenon, and the Taylor family attracted a great
deal of attention.

Die berühmten Vier. Die Vierlinge der Familie Taylor aus
Edmonton, London, hüpfen auf ihren Springstöcken die Straße
hinunter, 1958. Vierlingsgeburten waren damals sehr selten, und
die Taylor-Familie erregte große Aufmerksamkeit.

La célèbre bande des quatre. Les quadruplés Taylor d'Edmonton,
Londres, descendent la rue sur des échasses sauteuses, 1958.
Les quadruplés étaient un phénomène rare et la famille Taylor
suscitait beaucoup de curiosité.

Escaping the heat of a Roman
summer, 1950. Children splash in a
fountain created in a bygone age.

Auf der Flucht vor der Hitze eines
römischen Sommers, 1950. Kinder
planschen in einem Brunnen aus
längst vergangenen Tagen.

Comment fuir la chaleur d'un été
torride à Rome, 1950. Des enfants
s'amusent dans une fontaine
construite il y a bien longtemps.

Escaping the downpour of an English summer.
Holidaymakers shelter at Bournemouth pier
during the wet and dismal summer of 1954.

Auf der Flucht vor dem Wolkenbruch eines englischen Sommers. Urlauber suchen während des
verregneten Sommers von 1954 Schutz unter
dem Pier von Bournemouth.

Comment se protéger d'une averse en plein été
anglais. Des vacanciers se réfugient sous la jetée
de Bournemouth. L'été 1954 fut particulièrement
pluvieux et mauvais.

July 1950. A police sergeant keeps a watchful eye on
six performers from a charity matinée in aid of the Children's
League of Pity at the Saville Theatre, London.

Juli 1950. Ein Polizist behält sechs Mitwirkende einer
Aufführung im Londoner Saville Theatre zugunsten der
Children's League of Pity im Auge.

Juillet 1950. Un policier surveille attentivement six acteurs d'un
spectacle de charité en faveur de la Ligue de la pitié pour les
enfants au Saville Theatre, Londres.

Enid Blyton's *Noddy* inspects a contingent of 'Guards' outside Buckingham Palace, December 1959. They were members of the cast of the pantomime at the Prince's Theatre.

Enid Blytons berühmte *Nicky*-Figur inspiziert eine „Wache" vor dem Buckingham-Palast, Dezember 1959. Sie gehörten zu den Schauspielern eines Weihnachtsmärchens am Prince's Theatre.

Le *Oui-Oui* d'Enid Blyton, passant en revue les « gardes » de la reine, devant le Palais de Buckingham, décembre 1959. Ils faisaient partie d'une troupe qui jouait un spectacle de pantomime au Prince's Theatre.

Four astronauts line up in space suits, armed with their Dan Dare ray guns, 1952.
Dan Dare, hero of the *Eagle* comic, first published in the Fifties, was square-jawed,
invincible, and good-humoured – the very essence of an Englishman.

Vier Astronauten in Weltraumanzügen und mit Dan-Dare-Strahlenpistolen be-
waffnet, gehen in Verteidigungsposition, 1952. Der Held des *Eagle*-Comics, Dan
Dare, der erstmals in den fünfziger Jahren herausgegeben wurde, besaß ein breites
Kinn, war gutmütig und unbesiegbar – kurzum der Inbegriff eines Engländers.

Quatre enfants en tenue d'aéronaute et armés d'un fusil à rayon laser à la
Dan Dare, le héros d'*Eagle*, une bande dessinée publiée pour la première fois dans
les années cinquante, 1952. Ce personnage à la mâchoire carrée, invincible et
toujours de bonne humeur était l'essence même du véritable Anglais.

Inspection of a sentry at Horse Guards Parade, Whitehall, London, March 1959.

Inspektion einer Wache an der Horse Guards Parade, Whitehall, London, März 1959.

Inspection d'une sentinelle pendant le défilé de la Garde à cheval, Whitehall, Londres, mars 1959.

Gaining social skills. Miss Dorothy Winter guides 11-year-old Barry Hobbins through the complexities of ballroom dancing at the Odeon Cinema Ballroom, Edmonton, London, February 1958.

Das Erlernen gesellschaftlicher Umgangsformen. Miss Dorothy Winter führt den 11jährigen Barry Hobbins im Tanzsaal des Odeon-Kinos, Edmonton, London, in die Feinheiten des Gesellschaftstanzes ein, Februar 1958.

L'apprentissage des mondanités. Miss Dorothy Winter explique, tout en guidant Barry Hobbins, 11 ans, l'art de la danse dans la salle de bal du cinéma Odéon, Edmonton, Londres, février 1958.

Dress rehearsal. A 'babe' from the cast of the pantomime
Cinderella casts a critical eye over the pit orchestra at
Southall, London, January 1951.

Kostümprobe. Junge Mitwirkende des Weihnachtsmärchens
Cinderella begutachten kritisch das begleitende Orchester,
Southall, London, Januar 1951.

Répétition générale en costumes. Une fillette participant au
spectacle de *Cendrillon* observe d'un œil critique les
musiciens de l'orchestre, Southall, Londres, janvier 1951.

15. All human life
Menschliches, Allzumenschliches
Les petits et les grands événements de la vie

Cold War holiday, 1956. The back view of
two women on a beach in Germany,
sheltering from the elements with a home-
made windbreak.

Ferien während des Kalten Krieges, 1956.
Die Rückansicht zweier Damen an einem
deutschen Strand. Der improvisierte
Windschutz sollte sie offensichtlich vor der
rauhen Witterung bewahren.

Vacances au temps de la guerre froide, 1956.
Deux femmes, vues de derrière, sur une plage
en Allemagne. Un coupe-vent improvisé les
protège des éléments.

15. All human life
Menschliches, Allzumenschliches
Les petits et les grands événements de la vie

It was the last decade of the unchallenged old order. Only a minority questioned the rightness of corporal and capital punishment. The Lord's Day was strictly observed. Homosexuality was illegal. Illegitimacy was unacceptable. There was shame in divorcing. Children were seen and not heard. Hunting was regarded as part of a nation's glorious heritage. Whales were slaughtered. Forests were felled. Land, sea and air were recklessly polluted.

Against this backdrop of conformity, eccentrics continued to discover new and strange ways of behaving as everyday life unfolded around them. While the vast majority were concerned with the dramas of birth, death, poverty and starvation, there were those happy few who wanted to build bizarre gadgets, live in strange dwellings, eat unusual food.

Amateur scientists wired themselves to outlandish machines, claimed they were in contact with Martians, invented new 'cures' for old ailments. Pet owners taught their cats and dogs to perform curious and ungainly tricks. Inventive cranks sought innovative ways of proving that they were the strongest, the toughest, the fastest creatures on earth.

And all around, the masses feasted on the sight of the rich and famous behaving as they had always done.

Dies war das letzte Jahrzehnt, in dem die althergebrachten Werte und Normen nicht angezweifelt wurden. Nur eine kleine Minderheit stellte die Prügel- und die Todesstrafe in Frage. Der Tag des Herrn wurde als Ruhetag strikt befolgt. Homosexualität war strafbar. Uneheliche Kinder waren unakzeptabel und Scheidung war eine Schande. Kinder durfte man nur sehen, aber nicht hören. Die Jagd war Teil des glorreichen Erbes der Nation. Wale wurden abgeschlachtet, Wälder abgeholzt und Land, Meer und Luft rücksichtslos verschmutzt.

Doch vor dem Hintergrund dieser Konformität entwickelten Exzentriker auch weiterhin neue und seltsame Verhaltensweisen. Während der Alltag seinen Lauf nahm und die große

1ehrheit der Bevölkerung sich mit den menschlichen Dramen von Geburt, Tod, Armut und
lunger befaßte, gab es immer noch einige Unverbesserliche, die bizarre Geräte bauen, in
genartigen Behausungen wohnen oder ungewöhnliche Dinge essen wollten.

Amateurwissenschaftler schlossen sich mit Kabeln an sonderbare Maschinen an, be-
aupteten, daß sie Kontakt zu Marsmenschen hätten, oder erfanden neue „Heilmittel" für
te Leiden. Besitzer von Haustieren brachten ihren Hunden und Katzen seltsame und
nelegante Kunststückchen bei, während einfallsreiche Spinner versuchten, auf stets
mnovative Art zu beweisen, daß sie die stärksten, die härtesten und die schnellsten Geschöpfe
er Welt seien.

Und überall auf der Welt ergötzten sich die Menschen an den Reichen und Berühmten, die
ch genau so verhielten, wie sie es schon immer getan hatten.

e fut la dernière décennie à ne pas remettre en cause l'ordre établi. Seule une minorité
interrogeait sur le bien-fondé du châtiment corporel et de la peine de mort. Le jour du Sei-
neur était strictement respecté, l'homosexualité illégale et l'illégitimité inacceptable.
ivorcer était une honte. Les enfants étaient tolérés parmi les adultes mais n'avaient pas leur
ot à dire. La chasse était considérée comme un prestigieux héritage national. Les baleines
aient massacrées, les forêts décimées. On polluait la terre, la mer et l'air sans arrière-pensée.

En marge de cette conformité ambiante, des excentriques persistaient à inventer de
ouveaux comportements bizarres dans la vie de tous les jours. Si la grande majorité des gens
ait préoccupée par les drames de la naissance, de la mort, de la pauvreté et de la famine, il y
vait encore des irréductibles ne songeant qu'à créer d'étranges gadgets, à vivre dans
'étonnantes maisons et manger des choses inhabituelles.

Les scientifiques amateurs se branchaient sur d'invraisemblables machines, prétendaient
tre en contact avec des Martiens et inventaient de nouveaux « remèdes » pour les maladies
nciennes. Les propriétaires d'animaux domestiques apprenaient à leurs chats et chiens des
uméros aussi curieux que disgracieux. Des inventeurs loufoques cherchaient à prouver par
us les moyens qu'ils étaient les plus forts, les plus coriaces ou les plus rapides de la planète.

Enfin, partout dans le monde, les masses observaient avec délice les frasques des gens
ches et célèbres pour qui rien ne semblait devoir changer.

Hollywood, 1954. Rin Tin Tin, the canine film star, surveys his fan mail. The first
Rin Tin Tin began life as a guard dog in the German army, became a silent film
star, and died in 1932. The dog in this picture was a television upstart.

Hollywood, 1954. Der Hunde-Filmstar Rin Tin Tin beantwortet seine Fanpost.
Der erste Darsteller des Rin Tin Tin war ein ehemaliger Wachhund der deutschen
Wehrmacht, der ins Stummfilmfach überwechselte und 1932 starb. Der Hund auf
dieser Aufnahme, war ein Double aus der Fernsehwelt.

Hollywood, 1954. Rin Tin Tin, le chien-vedette du cinéma, répond au courrier de
ses admirateurs. Le premier Rin Tin Tin commença comme chien de garde dans
l'armée allemande avant de devenir star de film muet. Il mourut en 1932. Le
chien ici photographié est une doublure pour la télévision.

London, December 1954. Susie the brown
bear rides the dodgems at the funfair
attached to Bertram Mills Circus, Olympia.

London, Dezember 1954. Der Braunbär
Susie fährt Autoskooter auf einem
Rummelplatz, des Bertram-Mills-Circus,
Olympia.

Londres, décembre 1954. Susie, l'ours
brun conduit une auto-tamponneuse à la
foire qui jouxte le cirque de Bertram
Mills, Olympia.

Fun in the sun. Leopard-skin chic at the bar of a holiday camp on Corfu, October 1954. Photograph by Kurt Hutton.

Spaß in der Sonne. Leopardenfell-Schick an der Bar eines Feriendorfs auf Korfu, Oktober 1954. Fotografiert von Kurt Hutton.

Les plaisirs du soleil. Maillot de bain très chic, en peau de léopard, pour boire un verre au bar d'un camp de vacances à Corfou, octobre 1954. Cliché de Kurt Hutton.

...in in the sauna. An ...tendant hands his ...ustomer a bunch of ...rch twigs, 1954.

...ual in der Sauna. ...n Besucher läßt ...ch ein Bündel ...rkenzweige geben, ...954.

...ouffrir au sauna. ...n employé remet ...i client une verge ...e bouleau, 1954.

Japan, 1950. 1,500 young men scrabble
to find two batons that have been thrown
among them. The hunt took place in total
darkness – the photograph was taken
by flashlight.

Japan, 1950. 1.500 junge Männer suchen
in völliger Dunkelheit fieberhaft nach
zwei Stäben, die in die Menschenmenge
geworfen worden sind – das Bild wurde
mit Blitzlicht aufgenommen.

Japon, 1950. 1 500 jeunes hommes pêle-
mêle à la recherche de deux matraques
jetées parmi eux. La scène se déroule dans
une obscurité totale – la photographie a
été prise avec un flash.

July 1959. A diver retrieves forged £5 notes from Lake Toplitz in the Austrian Alps. The notes had been printed by the Nazis during World War II as part of a plan to destabilize the British economy, but had been dumped in the lake.

Juli 1959. Ein Taucher hilft bei der Bergung gefälschter 5-Pfund-Noten aus dem Toplitzer See in den österreichischen Alpen. Die von den Nazis während des Zweiten Weltkrieges gedruckten und später in dem See versenkten Banknoten waren Teil eines Plans, der die britische Wirtschaft schwächen sollte.

Juillet 1959. Faux billets de 5 £ repêchés au fond du lac Topliz dans les Alpes autrichiennes. Ces billets, imprimés par les nazis pendant la Seconde Guerre mondiale pour déstabiliser l'économie britannique, avaient été jetés dans le lac.

The Amazing Randi, professional escapologist, at the West Ham Municipal Baths, London, October 1958. He was beginning an attempt to break his own underwater endurance record.

Der Sensationelle Randi, ein professioneller Entfesselungskünstler, in der städtischen Badeanstalt von West Ham, London, Oktober 1958. Er unternimmt einen Versuch, seinen eigenen Unterwasserrekord zu brechen.

Le Formidable Randi, virtuose professionnel de l'évasion, photographié aux bains municipaux de West Ham, va tenter de battre son propre record de temps passé sous l'eau, Londres, octobre 1958.

Dumb waiter.
An Alsatian balance
a set of cups and
saucers on his head,
1954. Don't
ask why.

Stummer Diener.
Ein Schäferhund
balanciert vier
Tassen und
Untertassen auf
seinem Kopf, 1954.
Fragen Sie
nicht, warum.

Serviteur muet.
Un berger allemand
avançant avec quatr
tasses et sous-tasses
posées sur la tête,
1954. Allez
savoir pourquoi.

Clever artist. Fred
Lony of Latvia
balances 22 chairs
between his teeth at
Tom Arnold's
Circus, Harringay,
London, December
1956.

Geschickter Artist.
Der Lette Fred Lony
balanciert 22 Stühle
mit den Zähnen im
Tom Arnold's
Circus, Harringay,
London, Dezember
1956.

Brillant numéro au
cirque Tom Arnold à
Harringay, Londres,
décembre 1956.
Fred Lony,
originaire de
Lettonie, tient entre
ses dents 22 chaises
en équilibre.

London, 1953.
Two acrobats
present their own
way of advertising
Bertram Mills
Circus,
Hammersmith
Broadway.

London, 1953.
Zwei Akrobatinnen
werben auf ihre gar
persönliche Art für
den Bertram Mills
Circus, Hammer-
smith Broadway.

Londres, 1953.
Deux acrobates
font à leur manière
la publicité du
cirque de Bertram
Mills, Hammersmit
Broadway.

Japanese acrobat
Gyokusho Terajima
interrupts a family
dinner to perform
a handstand on his
brother Chame's
head, 1956.

Der japanische
Akrobat Gyokusho
Terajima unterbricht
die Mahlzeit im
Familienkreis, um
einen Handstand auf
dem Kopf seines
Bruders Chame aus-
zuführen, 1956.

L'acrobate japonais
Gyokusho Terajima
interrompt un
repas familial pour
exécuter un numéro
d'équilibre sur la
tête de son frère
Chame, 1956.

Boys from a naval training school rehearse
for their part in the Gravesend May Queen
Carnival, Kent, May 1950.

Junge Kadetten einer Marineschule proben
für ihren Auftritt beim Maskenfest der
Maikönigin in Gravesend, Kent, Mai 1950.

Des étudiants de l'Ecole navale répètent leur
numéro pour le carnaval de la reine de mai à
Gravesend, Kent, mai 1950.

Animal trainer Robert Baudy fits lion masks on his team of boxer dogs, 1956. Dogs were cheaper and easier to train than lions, and the audience responded just as enthusiastically.

Der Dompteur Robert Baudy schnallt seinen Boxerhunden Löwenmasken um, 1956. Es war billiger und leichter Hunde zu trainieren als Löwen, und sie fanden beim Publikum ebensoviel Anklang.

Le dompteur Robert Baudy ajuste un masque de lion sur ses boxers, 1956. Il était moins coûteux et plus facile d'entraîner des chiens plutôt que des lions et le public était tout aussi enthousiaste.

In the wings of a theatre, a charlady joins in a group dance audition, June 1956.

In den Kulissen eine Theaters schließt sich eine Putzfrau der Gruppe der Vortanzenden an, Juni 1956.

Dans les coulisses d'un théâtre, une femme de ménage se joint aux danseuses auditionnées, juin 1956.

Liverpool
housewives scrub
their front
doorsteps, April
1954. To have a
dirty 'step' was a
sign of slovenliness.

Liverpooler Haus-
frauen schrubben
die Stufen ihres
Hauseingangs,
April 1954. Einen
schmutzigen
Eingang zu haben,
war ein Zeichen von
Nachlässigkeit.

Des ménagères de
Liverpool nettoient
leur pas de porte,
avril 1954. Une
« marche » sale était
un signe de négli-
gence.

More nourishing than a packet of crisps, more ridiculous than Monty Python. Circus performer Millie Kayes swallows the head of a 12ft python in the bar of the Peggy Bradford Hotel, 1952.

Nahrhafter als eine Tüte Kartoffelchips und noch absurder als Monty Python. Die Zirkusartistin Millie Kayes schluckt in der Bar des Peggy Bradford Hotels den Kopf einer dreieinhalb Meter langen Python, 1952.

Plus nourrissant qu'un paquet de chips, plus ridicule qu'un Monty Python. Millie Kayes, artiste de cirque, avale la tête d'un python de 3,5 mètres de long au bar de l'hôtel Peggy Bradford, 1952.

October 1950. Anne Fenton and her grey mare, Anita, share a round of drinks at the Hotel Marazion, Cornwall. The horse was subsequently stopped by police and prosecuted for drunken driving when its nosebag turned green.

Oktober 1950. Anne Fenton und ihr Apfelschimmel Anita genießen eine feucht-fröhliche Runde im Hotel Marazion, Cornwall. Das Pferd wurde wenig später von der Polizei angehalten und wurde wegen Trunkenheit im Verkehr verwarnt, als sich sein Futtersack grün verfärbte.

Octobre 1950. Anne Fenton et sa jument grise, Anita, boivent un verre à l'hôtel Marazion, Cornouailles. Le cheval fut arrêté un peu plus tard par la police et condamné pour conduite en état d'ivresse, son sac d'avoine étant devenu vert.

An entire house is moved along railway tracks at Rueil-Malmaison, Paris, 1955. Since it occupied all the lines leading to and from the Gare St Lazare, it is to be hoped that this wasn't during rush hour.

Ein komplettes Haus wird in Rueil-Malmaison, Paris, über Eisenbahn-schienen transportiert, 1955. Da es sämtliche vom und zum Bahnhof St. Lazare führenden Gleise blockierte, bleibt nur zu hoffen, daß die Rush-hour davon nicht betroffen war.

Une maison entière déplacée sur des rails à Rueil-Malmaison, Paris, 1955. Etant donné qu'elle occupait toutes les voies menant à la gare Saint-Lazare, on peut espérer que l'opération avait lieu en dehors des heures de pointe.

May 1959. A stuffed giraffe, weighing half a ton, is manoeuvred into the Natural History Museum in South Kensington, London.

Mai 1959. Eine ausgestopfte Giraffe mit dem Gewicht einer halben Tonne wird durch den Eingang des Naturkundemuseums in South Kensington, London, manövriert.

Mai 1959. Une girafe empaillée, pesant une demi-tonne, est transportée à l'intérieur du musée d'histoire naturelle de South Kensington, Londres.

Florida, 1959. A diver vacuums the algae from the floor of the Miami Seaquarium. The job had to be done at least five times a week.

Florida, 1959. Ein Taucher entfernt die Algenablagerung vom Boden des Meeresaquariums in Miami. Diese Reinigungsaktion mußte mindestens fünfmal in der Woche durchgeführt werden.

Floride, 1959. Un plongeur aspire les algues de l'Aquarium de Miami. Cette tâche devait être exécutée au moins cinq fois par semaine.

ndon, 1950.
eper Jones douses
flock of penguins
the Regent's Park
o.

ndon, 1950.
erwärter Jones
wärt seiner Schar
Pinguinen im
gent's Park Zoo
e Dusche.

ndres, 1950. Le
dien, M. Jones,
sse à la douche
troupeau
pingouins au zoo
Regent's Park.

Will Lambert stand
on Anthony Biddle,
1956. Lambert
weighed 186
pounds. Biddle was
a millionaire
sportsman with
great faith in the
Lord.

Will Lambert steht
auf Anthony Biddle
1956. Lambert wog
93 Kilogramm.
Biddle war ein
sportlicher Million.
mit großem Gott-
vertrauen.

Will Lambert,
debout sur Anthon
Biddle, 1956.
Lambert pesait 93
kilos. Biddle
était un sportif
millionnaire et un
fervent croyant.

Vagn Hansen's photograph of a member of the Vikings Swimming Club, 1955. Club members were prepared to swim in icy water.

Ein Sportler des Wikinger-Schwimmvereins, fotografiert von Vagn Hansen, 1955. Die Vereinsmitglieder ließen sich auch von den eisigsten Wassertemperaturen nicht abschrecken.

Un nageur du club de natation des Vikings photographié par Vagn Hansen, 1955. Les membres du club avaient l'habitude de nager dans une eau glacée.

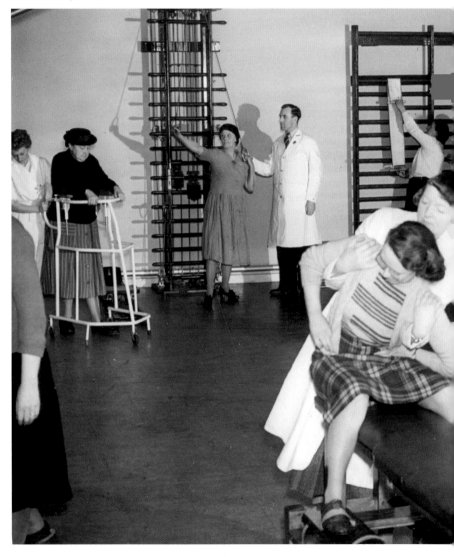

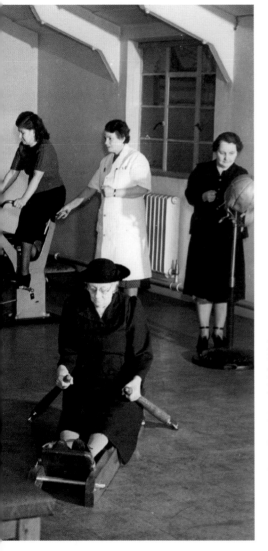

February 1950. The gymnasium at St Olave's Hospital, Rotherhithe, London. These were the great and glorious early days of the National Health Service and free medical treatment in Britain.

Februar 1950. Die Turnhalle des St. Olave's Hospitals, Rotherhithe, London. Dies waren die frühen, glorreichen Tage des Staatlichen Gesundheitsdienstes und der kostenlosen medizinischen Betreuung in Großbritannien.

Février 1950. Gymnase de l'hôpital Saint Olave, Rotherhithe, Londres. C'était la grande et glorieuse époque de la Sécurité Sociale et des soins médicaux gratuits pour tous en Grande-Bretagne.

Charles Hewitt's study of the inner workings of a marriage bureau,
November 1955. A prospective groom examines the photograph of
a potential bride.

Eine Studie der internen Abläufe eines Eheanbahnungsinstituts von
Charles Hewitt, November 1955. Ein hoffnungsvoller Aspirant
begutachtet das Porträt einer potentiellen Braut.

Le fonctionnement d'une agence matrimoniale saisi par Charles
Hewitt, novembre 1955. Un mari potentiel examine la
photographie d'une épouse potientelle.

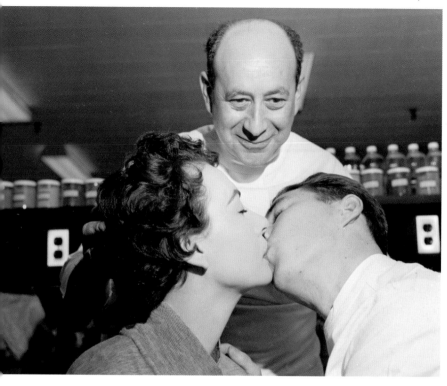

A laboratory technician gets voyeuristic pleasure from watching a couple test the durability of lipstick at the Helena Rubinstein Laboratories, East Hills, California, 1950.

Ein Labortechniker beobachtet mit voyeuristischem Pläsier ein Pärchen, das die Kußechtheit von Lippenstiften prüft, Helena Rubinstein Laboratorien, East Hills, Kalifornien, 1950.

Un laborantin observe avec un plaisir de voyeur un couple en train de tester la tenue d'un rouge à lèvres aux laboratoires Helena Rubinstein, East Hills, Californie, 1950.

May 1953. Pipe-Major Sardar Khan of the 1st Punjab Regiment rehearses outside the BBC Studios in London's West End.

Mai 1953. Dudelsackspieler Major Sardar Khan vom 1. Pandschabischen Regiment probt vor den Studios der BBC im Londoner West End.

Mai 1953. Sardar Kahn, cornemuseur du 1er régiment du Punjab, en répétition devant les studios de la BBC dans le West End de Londres.

Scotland, August
1954. Edith Barlow,
32 inches high, and
reputedly smallest
woman in the world,
attracts a crowd of
shoppers in Dundee.

Schottland, August
1954. Edith Barlow,
die mit einer
Körpergröße von
knapp 56 cm als
kleinste Frau der
Welt galt, erregt in
Dundee einiges
Aufsehen unter den
Passanten.

Écosse, août 1954.
Edith Barlow, haute
de 56 cm et connue
pour être la plus
petite femme du
monde, provoque
un attroupement de
badauds à Dundee.

Fire in mouth. A young fire-eater
takes time out to light his father's
cigarette, 1955.

Feuer im Mund. Ein junger Feuer-
schlucker unterbricht kurz seine Dar-
bietung, um seinem Vater eine Zigarette
anzuzünden, 1955.

Le feu à la bouche. Un jeune cracheur
de feu prend le temps d'allumer une
cigarette à son père, 1955.

Heart in mouth. The journalist Macdonald Hastings standing in as a knife thrower's target, 1951. This was one of many dangers Hastings faced for a series of magazine articles.

Herzklopfen. Der Journalist Macdonald Hastings dient einem Messerwerfer als Zielscheibe, 1951. Dies war nur eine von zahlreichen Gefahren, denen Hastings für eine Serie von Zeitschriftenartikeln ins Auge blickte.

Haut le cœur. Le journaliste Macdonald Hastings sert de cible à un lanceur de couteaux, 1951. Ce fut l'un des nombreux risques encourus par Hastings pour l'un de ses reportages.

September 1956. Douglas Barr models a satin-lined American opera cape in black silk and worsted, interwoven with gleaming jet lurex. He was attending the Lurex International Fair, to mark the tenth anniversary of the development of lurex.

September 1956. Douglas Barr präsentiert einen satingefütterten amerikanischen Opernumhang aus schwarzer Seide und Kammgarnstoff, verwebt mit schimmerndem, tiefschwarzem Lurexgarn. Er besuchte die Internationale Lurex-Messe anläßlich des zehnten Jahrestags der Entwicklung dieses Materials.

Septembre 1956. Douglas Barr, vêtu d'une cape d'opéra américaine en soie noire et en worsted, doublée de satin et tissée de lurex brillant. Il participait au Salon international du lurex qui commémorait le dixième anniversaire de l'invention de cette matière.

tting ready for
e parade ring at a
 show, 1952.

zte Vorbereitun-
n für den großen
ftritt auf einer
zenschau, 1952.

rnière retouche
nt de faire le tour
 podium lors d'un
on du chat, 1952.

'Truly the light is sweet...' (*Ecclesiastes* 11:7). But the 'nuns' here are actors taking a break from filming, July 1959.

„Süß ist das Licht ..." (*Prediger* 11,7). Doch diese „Nonnen" sind Schauspielerinnen, die während der Dreharbeiten eine Zigarettenpause einlegen, Juli 1959.

« Le feu est vraiment doux ... » (*Ecclésiaste* 11:7). Mais ces « nonnes » sont en fait des actrices faisant une pause loin du plateau, juillet 1959.

'Vows can't change nature, priests are only men…' (Robert Browning – *The Ring and the Book*). Seminarists at the St Ignatius Loyola shrine at Azpeitia, Guipyzloa, Spain, enjoy a game of basketball, 1955.

„Ein Schwur kann die Natur nicht verändern, Priester sind nur Menschen …" (Robert Browning – *Der Ring und das Buch*). Seminaristen des Schreins des Heiligen Ignatius von Loyola in Azpeitia, Guipyzloa, Spanien, vergnügen sich bei einem Basketballspiel, 1955.

« Les vœux ne peuvent changer la nature, les prêtres ne sont que des hommes … » (Robert Browning – *The Ring and the Book*). Des séminaristes prennent plaisir à jouer au basket à Azpeitia, le saint lieu de Saint Ignace Loyola, Espagne, 1955.

May 1954. (Left to right) Ethel Glizzard, Gertrude Price and Aimée Price at celebrations to mark the 80th anniversary of Croydon High School for Girls, near London.

Mai 1954. (Von links nach rechts) Ethel Glizzard, Gertrude Price und Aimée Price auf der 80-Jahr-Feier der Mädchen-Oberschule in Croydon bei London.

Mai 1954. (De gauche à droite) Ethel Glizzard, Gertrude Price et Aimée Price participent à la fête qui célèbre le 80e anniversaire de l'école des filles de Croydon High, près de Londres.

Bert Hardy's photograph of a fancy dress party in a house in Chelsea, 1952. Chelsea was then still seen as the Bohemian quarter of London.

Kostümfest in einem Haus in Chelsea fotografiert von Bert Hardy, 1952. Zu jener Zeit war Chelsea noch das Künstlerviertel in London.

Fête costumée dans une maison de Chelsea photographiée par Bert Hardy, 1952. A cette époque, Chelsea était encore le quartier bohème de Londres.

What the well-dressed 'flusher' was wearing in April 1950. Flushers were the men who maintained London's sewer system.

Die Ausstattung eines gut gekleideten „Spülers" im April 1950. Spüler waren für die Instandhaltung des Londoner Kanalisationssystems verantwortlich.

Voici la tenue du parfait éboueur, avril 1950. Cet homme faisait partie du corps des éboueurs affecté à la maintenance des égouts de Londres.

London, March 1954. A man wrapped in aluminium foil on his way to the Factory Equipment Exhibition at the Horticultural Halls.

London, März 1954. Ein in Aluminiumfolie bekleideter Mann auf dem Weg zur Ausstellung von Industrie-Equipment in den Hallen der Gartenschau.

Londres, mars 1954. Un homme vêtu d'une combinaison en aluminium se rend au Salon de l'équipement industriel aux Halles de l'horticulture.

October 1951.
Photographers
outside Buckingham
Palace await news of
the operation that
removed one of
George VI's lungs.

Oktober 1951.
Fotografen warten
vor dem Bucking-
ham-Palast auf
Neuigkeiten über
die Operation, in
der König Georg VI.
ein Lungenflügel
entfernt wurde.

Octobre 1951.
Photographes
devant le palais de
Buckingham dans
l'attente de
nouvelles après
l'opération au cours
de laquelle on enleva
un poumon au roi
Georges VI.

6 February 1952. Crowds at Buckingham Palace reading news of the death at Sandringham of King George VI. The King, who was a heavy cigarette smoker, had died of lung cancer.

6. Februar 1952. Menschenmengen versammeln sich vor dem Buckingham-Palast, um die Nachricht vom Tod König Georg VI. in Sandringham nachzulesen. Der König war jahrelang Kettenraucher gewesen und an Lungenkrebs gestorben.

6 février 1952. Des gens, parmi la foule réunie devant le palais de Buckingham, lisent le journal relatant le décès du roi Georges VI survenu à Sandringham. Le roi, grand fumeur de cigarettes, était mort d'un cancer des poumons.

February 1952. Members of the Royal Family at the funeral of
King George VI, Windsor. (From left to right) Queen Elizabeth II;
Queen Mary, mother of George VI; and Queen Elizabeth, the
dead King's widow.

Februar 1952. Angehörige der königlichen Familie während der
Beisetzung König Georgs VI., Windsor. (Von links nach rechts)
Königin Elisabeth II., Königin Maria, die Mutter Georgs VI., und
Königin Elisabeth, die Witwe des verstorbenen Königs.

Février 1952. Membres de la famille royale lors des funérailles du
roi Georges VI, Windsor. (De gauche à droite) la reine Elisabeth
II, la reine Marie, mère de Georges VI, et la reine Elisabeth, la
veuve du roi défunt.

August 1952.
Children in Stepney,
East London, read a
poster detailing
plans for a street
party to celebrate
the Coronation of
Elizabeth II.

August 1952. Kinder
in Stepney, Ost-
London, lesen ein
Plakat, auf dem die
Einzelheiten eines
Straßenfestes be-
kanntgegeben
werden, das am Tag
der Krönung Elisa-
beth II. stattfinden
sollte.

Août 1952. Des
enfants du quartier
de Stepney, à l'est
de Londres, lisent
l'affiche annonçant
le programme de la
fête de rue qui aura
lieu le jour du cou-
ronnement de la
reine Elisabeth II.

une 1953. The
wning moment
Westminster
pey. The
rhbishop of
nterbury raises
crown above the
ereign's head.

uni 1953. Der
oment der Krö-
ng in der Abtei
1 Westminster.
r Erzbischof von
nterbury setzt die
one auf das Haupt
r Monarchin.

uin 1953. Scène
couronnement à
obaye de West-
nster. L'arche-
que de Canterbury
ce la couronne
r la tête de la
uveraine.

The aftermath of a street party in Fulham, London on Coronation Day, 1953. The hope was that the young Queen would inspire a new and glorious Elizabethan Age, but the hangover came first.

Die Nachwirkungen eines Straßenfestes in Fulham, London, am Krönungstag, 1953. Die Nation hoffte, daß mit der Regentschaft der jungen Königin ein neues, glorreiches elisabethanisches Zeitalter anbrechen werde, doch zuerst einmal mußte der Kater überstanden werden.

Suites d'une fête de rue à Fulham, Londres, le jour du couronnement, 1953. L'espoir était grand de voir la jeune reine inspirer un nouvel âge de gloire élisabéthaine mais celui-ci n'en débuta pas moins par une gueule de bois.

woman in
orpeth Street,
st London, cleans
r front steps for
izabeth's
oronation.

ne Frau in der
orpeth Street, Ost-
ndon, reinigt und
hmückt ihren
auseingang für die
rönungsfeierlich-
iten Elisabeths II.

ne femme sur
orpeth Street dans
st de Londres
ttoyant ses
caliers pour le
uronnement
Elisabeth.

The Coronation party in Morpeth Street, London, 2 June 1953. The Coronation itself was televised, but few people in Britain had television sets at that time, so communities got together in streets that were still free of motor cars.

Das Straßenfest anläßlich der Krönung in der Morpeth Street, London, 2. Juni 1953. Die Krönung selbst wurde zwar im Fernsehen übertragen, doch zu jener Zeit besaß noch kaum jemand einen Fernsehapparat. So kamen die Leute auf den damals noch autofreien Straßen zum Feiern zusammen.

La fête du couronnement à Morpeth Street, Londres, 2 juin 1953. La cérémonie fut retransmise à la télévision. Mais à cette époque, rares étaient les gens qui possédaient un téléviseur et les habitants se retrouvèrent dans la rue – à l'époque dépourvue de voitures – pour la fête.

Two girls from the East End of London dance in the street on Coronation Day, 1953. Though the day itself was cold and damp, the celebrations continued until well into the night.

Zwei Mädchen aus dem Londoner East End tanzen am Krönungstag auf der Straße, 1953. Trotz der feuchtkalten Witterung, die an jenem Tag herrschte, feierten die Menschen bis spät in die Nacht hinein.

Deux petites filles de l'est de Londres dansent dans la rue le jour du couronnement, 1953. Malgré la pluie et le froid qu'il fit ce jour-là, les célébrations se déroulèrent jusque tard dans la nuit.

Senator John F
Kennedy and
Jacqueline Lee
Bouvier march
down the aisle at th
end of their weddir
ceremony at
Newport, Rhode
Island, 15
September 1953.

Senator John F.
Kennedy und
Jacqueline Lee
Bouvier verlassen
nach der Trauungs-
zeremonie die
Kirche in Newport,
Rhode Island, 15.
September 1953.

Le sénateur John F.
Kennedy et
Jacqueline Lee
Bouvier descendent
l'allée de l'église
après la cérémonie
de leur mariage à
Newport, Rhode
Island, 15 septembr
1953.

The wedding of Grace Kelly and Prince Rainier, Monaco Cathedral, 19 April 1956. They met while she was filming *To Catch a Thief* a year earlier.

Die Hochzeit von Grace Kelly und Fürst Rainier in der Kathedrale von Monaco, 19. April 1956. Ein Jahr zuvor hatten sie sich bei Kellys Dreharbeiten zu *Über den Dächern von Nizza* kennengelernt.

Le mariage de Grace Kelly et du prince Rainier à la cathédrale de Monaco, 19 avril 1956. Ils s'étaient rencontrés sur le tournage de *La main au collet*, un an plus tôt.

ndex

gettyimages

Over 70 million images and 30,000 hours of film footage are held by the various collections owned by Getty Images. These cover a vast number of subjects from the earliest photojournalism to current press photography, sports, social history and geography. Getty Images' conceptual imagery is renowned amongst creative end users.
www.gettyimages.com

Über 70 Millionen Bilder und 30 000 Stunden Film befinden sich in den verschiedenen Archiven von Getty Images. Sie decken ein breites Spektrum an Themen ab – von den ersten Tagen des Fotojournalismus bis hin zu aktueller Pressefotografie, Sport, Sozialgeschichte und Geographie. Bei kreativen Anwendern ist das Material von Getty Images für seine ausdrucksstarke Bildsprache bekannt.
www.gettyimages.com

Plus de 70 millions d'images et 30 000 heures de films sont détenus par les différentes collections dont Getty Images est le propriétaire. Cela couvre un nombre considérable de sujets – des débuts du photojournalisme aux photographies actuelles de presse, de sport, d'histoire sociale et de géographie. Le concept photographique de Getty Images est reconnu des créatifs.
www.gettyimages.com

Acknowledgements

Alan Band 35, 362
Daniel Farson 190, 193-4